THE LEADER
IN
TELEPHONE RACING

COMMENTARIES

MAINLINE

0898·500·300

All the action from all the courses on just one number

INDIVIDUAL COURSE COMMENTARIES
0898·500·PLUS

Course Number available in Daily and Racing Press

COMMENTARY CALL-UP
0898·500·368

Missed a live race commentary? Dial into the Racecall Daily
Commentary Library and follow the computer instructions for
a re-run of the race of your choice.

RESULTS

COURSE LINES

Results from just the one course, starting with
the most recent race.

RESULTS FLASH
0898·500·350

A rapid round-up from all meetings starting with the latest race and
working backwards through the day.

CLASSIFIED
0898·500·345

Complete course by course results service.

THE MOST COMPREHENSIVE SERVICE AVAILABLE

TIS plc., 24 West Smithfield, London EC1A 9DL. Calls cost 36p per minute cheap rate and 48p per minute at all other times

AMARI KING
AMONG FRIENDS
ARPAL BREEZE
AUTHORSHIP (USA)
BALLINROSTIG
BLUE BOURBON
BONANZA
BOUTZDAROFF
BUCK WILLOW
CHERRYKINO
CRYSTAL SPIRIT
DAWSON CITY
DERRING VALLEY
FISHKI
GLENBROOK D'OR
GOLD CAP (FR)
GREEK FLUTTER
HAITHAM
IAMA ZULU
JODAMI
KINGS FOUNTAIN
LAUNDRYMAN
MACARTHUR
MONUMENTAL LAD
MORLEY STREET
MR MONDAY
MUSE
MUTARE
NEW YORK RAINBOW
OBIE'S TRAIN
O'REILLY
PAPERWORK BOY
PARTY POLITICS
PLAT REAY
PRIME DISPLAY (USA)
QUENTIN DURWOOD
REMITTANCE MAN
RHODES
ROMANY KING
RONANS BIRTHDAY
ROSS VENTURE
ROYAL ASTRONAUT (USA)
SHANNON GLEN
TARDA
TREFELYN CONE
UNSHAKEABLE
VICOMPT DE VALMONT
WELSHMAN
WONDER MAN (FR)
YOUNG BENZ

AMARI KING

7 b.g. Sit In The Corner (USA)
Maywell (Harwell)

Quantity rather than quality was the order of the day at Stratford's April meeting, but the afternoon featured two impressive winning performances—that of Castle Secret in a division of the stayers' novice hurdle and Amari King in the two-mile handicap chase. Whereas Castle Secret went on to win another race, Amari King didn't run again, being retired for the season with a record of three victories (one when amateur ridden) in five starts. Amari King really was impressive. In a race run at a good pace, he was always going well; he quickened clear two out having jumped into the lead three out, and was so much on top of the twelve-length runner-up Guiburn's Nephew on the run-in that the jockey was able to be very easy on him. Amari King has not been taken to task by the official handicapper for his performance, so we are happy to retain him for another season as a chaser to follow and look forward to seeing him develop further. Two miles is his trip, the more strongly-run the race the better, as he is invariably held up. He acts on soft going. **Capt. T. A. Forster**

AMONG FRIENDS

6 b.g. Green Shoon
Lin-A-Dee (Linacre)

This half-brother to the fair hurdler Swanee Prince was quite well regarded among his stable's young horses last season. Not without good reason on the racecourse evidence available, though they flew too high with him on occasions—as when taking on Stratford Ponds second time up at Cheltenham in November and Shannon Glen and company in the Mumm Prize Novices' Hurdle at Liverpool in April. Among Friends showed promise first time out when fourth in a big field of novices at Newbury; he showed rateable form on nearly all his subsequent outings, including when joint-favourite for a twenty-three-runner novices' handicap at Newbury in March (he finished fifth there behind Wagon Load). Yet for all his efforts Among Friends ended the campaign still a maiden. You can be sure that if he keeps fit and well he'll get off the mark in 1991/2, in novice or handicap company, at up to two and a half miles. Indeed, we anticipate that he won't stop at one win, and that he'll turn out as good over hurdles as his half-brother. His best form so far has been shown on dead going. **G. B. Balding**

ARPAL BREEZE

6 ch.g. Deep Run
Arpal Magic (Master Owen)

In the words of his trainer 'Arpal Breeze's future lies over fences; he's big, he's strong and he jumps well. He'll be a nice chaser in the autumn'. Arpal Breeze won a two-mile novice hurdle at Kelso in November on his first appearance last season. The manner in which he accounted for the runner-up Lothian Captain suggested he'd follow up in similar company, but he was beaten in his four remaining races,

4

performing below expectations in the last three, all three run on ground softer than at Kelso. Arpal Breeze seemed not to get home when tackling two and three quarter miles on dead, nor when tackling two and a half on very heavy. Maybe he'll prove best at two miles, but we think there's a good chance that he'll get two and a half so long as conditions aren't testing; the evidence so far suggests that he is best on a sound surface. He should win novice chases in the North. **G. Richards**

AUTHORSHIP (USA) **| 5 b. or br.g. Balzac (USA)**
| Piap (USA) (L'Aiglon (USA))

Given a thorough test of stamina over hurdles, Authorship may well have more improvement in him. Although he has won over the minimum trip, he's shown improved form every time he's been raised in distance, and on his final start in 1990/1 he put up a good effort to finish eight lengths second to the much-improved Tapageur in a two-and-three-quarter-mile event at Stratford in May. He'd run creditably on all five of his previous starts of the season, winning conditional jockeys handicaps at Cheltenham and Newbury. On the latter course he put up an extraordinary performance to beat Stage Player by two lengths, coming from a seemingly-impossible position to lead on the flat and win going away. For a horse who stays well he has a respectable turn of foot, which will make him a useful proposition in staying handicap hurdles in 1991/2. He's shown himself still to be in good heart since Stratford, winning a long-distance handicap on the Flat at Pontefract and finishing an excellent fifth to Cabochon in another at Royal Ascot, showing much improved form. As on the Flat, Authorship is well suited by a sound surface over jumps, and acts on firm ground. **W. J. Musson**

BALLINROSTIG **| 8 ch.g. General Ironside**
| Mavar's Choice (Virginia Boy)

When the ground is riding fast, Ballinrostig looks one to be on in middle-of-the-road stayers' handicaps in the North. A winning point-to-pointer in Ireland, he was exported from his native country prior to the 1990/1 season. He showed plenty of ability in his first four starts in Britain, though twice falling in the closing stages when holding every chance, and he really came to prominence when racing on a firm surface for the first time on his fifth start. That race, a novice handicap chase at Doncaster in January, was quite a well-contested affair, but Ballinrostig made it look very one-sided, quickening on the run-in and beating Hey Rawley by ten lengths. The following month Ballinrostig was returned to Doncaster to contest a non-handicap under similar conditions. He impressed again in beating Quick Reaction by twenty lengths, his task having been made easier by the departure of the other joint-favourite Tug of Gold. Returned to a soft surface for his remaining two outings, Ballinrostig failed to maintain his improvement, coming a modest last of five finishers in a well-contested handicap at Newcastle, and pulled up when facing a stiff task in the Mumm Club Novices' Chase at Liverpool. Ballinrostig, who stays three miles well and jumps soundly, looks likely to get back on the winning trail when returned to fast ground conditions. **Denys Smith**

BLUE BOURBON
7 b.g. Ile de Bourbon (USA)
Habanna (Habitat)

Blue Bourbon made a satisfactory start to his chasing career last season, winning at Warwick on his debut and running some good races in defeat. He quickened nicely on the run-in when beating Teniente by five lengths at Warwick, and also showed pace when runner-up on the same course and at Stratford. At Stratford, Blue Bourbon was the only runner able remotely to threaten the very useful Last 'o' the Bunch in the latter stages, while on his return to Warwick he was worn down only close home by Roxall Clump, having had most of his rivals in trouble soon after jumping into the lead at the seventh. But for a fall two out at Newton Abbot, Blue Bourbon would probably have ended the season with a victory, for he was about three lengths clear at the time and still travelling quite well. Blue Bourbon, who acts on heavy going, will start the season on a fair mark, and he looks sure to win two-mile handicaps around the minor tracks. **R. J. Holder**

BONANZA
4 ch.g. Glenstal (USA)
Forliana (Forli (ARG))

Only Pipe, Richards, Stephenson and Gifford trained more winners than Mary Reveley in the 1990/1 National Hunt season, when fifty-eight races were won by her Saltburn stable. It's a stable which goes from strength to strength, and we wouldn't care to bet against it improving on that total this time. One horse who looks likely to make another significant contribution is Bonanza, successful on all three of his starts after being bought for 6,000 guineas at the Doncaster November Sales. A winner of a two-and-a-half mile seller at Sedgefield earlier that month, Bonanza, raced only at two miles by his new connections, showed himself much better than a plater. Following victories in

❚ Bonanza still has ground to make up on Sir Peter Lely

claiming events at Catterick, Bonanza won the Northern Champion Juvenile Handicap Hurdle at Newcastle by one and a half lengths from Sir Peter Lely, the pair clear of top-weight Montpelier Lad and four others. Tapped for pace after the third last, Bonanza stayed on strongly in the straight and caught Sir Peter Lely halfway up the run-in. Further improvement from Bonanza can be expected when he's returned to longer distances, and he'll pay his way in handicap company in the North. Bonanza raced only on good to soft ground apart from when beaten on good to firm on his hurdling debut. **Mrs G. R. Reveley**

BOUTZDAROFF I 9 ch.g. Dubassoff (USA)
Love Seat (King's Bench)

One of the best novice chasers of 1989/90, Boutzdaroff must have disappointed connections by managing only one win in the latest campaign, and that in a contest of no great consequence at Perth in April. But, by our reckoning, he'll soon put matters right. Boutzdaroff did more than enough in that one run to convince us that he'd indeed gone the right way and that presently he's better than is appreciated by the official handicapper.

Part of the problem for Boutzdaroff was that he got few opportunities to show what he could do. He completed four times out of just five attempts, giving the impression the race would do him good on one occasion and having ground conditions against him on another. Boutzdaroff disappointed only once, when third under top weight at Cheltenham in April, and he more than made up for that at Perth less than a week later. Giving weight to his four rivals in the RMC Catherwood Limited 'Little Bay' Handicap Chase, Boutzdaroff was backed to favouritism and gave his supporters scarcely a moment's cause for concern, leading before the fourth-last (which he hit) and soon pulling clear. At the line he had twelve lengths to spare over the

**I Boutzdaroff wins easily
I at Perth**

quite useful Clever Folly. Surprisingly, Boutzdaroff was raised only 2 lb in the official ratings for that success, despite the subsequent win of the runner-up. We feel that the official assessment underestimates Boutzdaroff to the tune of some 10 lb and as such he's merely going to need ordinary luck to win a good handicap or two along the way. The conditions Boutzdaroff requires to show his best are well-established by now. He's best at two miles on a sound surface—the ground at Perth was good. He usually jumps well, though he's shown a tendency to jump to his right in the closing stages. **J. G. FitzGerald**

BUCK WILLOW | 7 b.g. Kambalda
Da Capo (Kabale)

Jim Joel's black and scarlet colours continue to figure prominently on the National Hunt scene, and it surely won't be long before they're carried to victory by one of Mr Joel's more recent acquisitions, Buck Willow. A fair hurdler in Ireland, Buck Willow had three outings over fences last season for his present owner, showing such promise on the first two occasions that he was allowed to take his chance against Remittance Man and company in the Arkle Trophy at Cheltenham. Buck Willow's lack of experience showed in that hotly-contested race—he was well behind when brought down four out—but that won't be a problem in the coming season. He'll have more experience of fences than most of the horses he'll be meeting in novice chases, and he needs only to reproduce the form he showed when runner-up on his first two starts to win races. Beaten three lengths by My Young Man at Newbury on his chasing debut, Buck Willow then went down by four lengths to the smart Uncle Ernie at Ascot, on each occasion finishing a distance clear of the remainder. Though he races rather freely at present, Buck Willow will probably stay two and a half miles. Judged on his breeding he should be suited by the trip. His sire Kambalda, a very smart performer on the Flat, needed long distances to be seen to best advantage, while his half-brother Dusky Duke (by Dusky Boy) showed useful form at up to two and three quarter miles over fences. Buck Willow, a rangy, good sort, probably acts on any going. **J. T. Gifford**

CHERRYKINO | 6 b.g. Relkino
Cherry Stack (Raise You Ten)

When 'Cherry' appears in a jumper's pedigree nowadays you can be more or less certain that the horse in question is a relative of Arkle. The six-year-old gelding Cherrykino is no exception. His dam is a daughter of a half-sister to the brilliant Irish chaser. We don't for a minute expect that Cherrykino will come anywhere near matching his illustrious ancestor, but there's no doubt he's a useful sort in the making. Following an outing in a National Hunt Flat Race in 1989/90, Cherrykino progressed throughout his first season over hurdles, winning three of his four races, novice events at Hereford in November, Wincanton (a handicap) in January and Uttoxeter in April. He put up a fair performance on the last-named course, beating Forget The Rest by five lengths: pushed along from the fourth last in the three-mile contest, he stayed on to lead after the second last, and, despite hanging right and slightly hampering the runner-up at the final flight, he found extra on the run-in and won going away. As his pedigree suggests, Cherrykino is well suited by a test of stamina. Whether he's again campaigned over hurdles or, even better, switched to fences, Cherrykino looks assured of more success in the coming season. **Capt. T. A. Forster**

CRYSTAL SPIRIT
4 b.g. Kris
Crown Treasure (USA) (Graustark)

By the time you read this Crystal Spirit may well be one of the favourites for the Cesarewitch. He's quite useful on the Flat and capable of winning such a prize, but he's so much better over jumps that that's where his future really lies. Crystal Spirit took very well to hurdling in 1990/1 and already has two Grade 1 wins at Cheltenham to his credit, in the Bishops Cleeve Hurdle and the Sun Alliance Novices' Hurdle, both over two and a half miles. His defeat of older horses, including Mutare and Yorkshire Holly, in the Bishops Cleeve in January put him in with a great chance in the Sun Alliance, in which he (2/1) and the unbeaten Irish mare Minorettes Girl (4/1) dominated the betting in a field of twenty-nine. Two out in the Sun Alliance the pair were disputing the lead. Then Crystal Spirit gradually got on top, staying on strongly to beat his main rival pushed out by four lengths. At this point Crystal Spirit had taken his record to four wins from five starts and looked a good bet to improve it in the Mumm Prize Novices' Hurdle at Liverpool, but he was beaten there by Shannon Glen after failing to jump with his usual fluency. Why he should have been below his best is hard to pinpoint—most likely because he'd been on the go for a long time.

On his two performances at Cheltenham Crystal Spirit was clearly among last season's best novices. Furthermore he's very much more robust than the usual recruit from Flat racing and seems sure to train on. We think he'll develop into a top-class staying hurdler, and, in the longer term, make a chaser. At this stage connections may be thinking of going for the Champion Hurdle. It's doubtful he'll have the speed for that, though—Hopscotch proved too nippy for him over two miles in the Finale Junior Hurdle at Chepstow on his second outing—and he's likely to need at least two and a half to be seen to best advantage. Crystal Spirit must be one of the best-bred animals on the jumping circuit, being a half-brother to Glint of Gold and Diamond Shoal, who between them won nine Group 1 races on the Flat. With two Grade 1 wins over hurdles, Crystal Spirit is doing his bit for the family; and there are more to come. **I. A. Balding**

DAWSON CITY
4 ch.g. Glint of Gold
Lola Sharp (Sharpen Up)

Dawson City's first season over hurdles amounted to just four outings but he showed plenty of promise on each occasion and looks the type to go on improving. Following a five-length second to Native Mission in the Wensleydale Juvenile Hurdle at Wetherby in November on his hurdling debut, Dawson City easily landed the odds in ordinary juvenile events on the same course later that month and in December, in the latter race beating Reve de Valse by three and a half lengths. Dawson City was then upgraded and contested the Finale Junior Hurdle at Chepstow later in December, the most strongly-contested race for juveniles in the first half of the season, losing no caste in finishing third behind the clear winner Hopscotch and Crystal Spirit. Dawson City had been ridden from the front when winning both times at Wetherby, and would perhaps have fared better ridden more positively at Chepstow. He wasn't seen out again, but he's reportedly back in training for the 1991/2 season. Two-mile handicaps would seem ideal targets for him, and he looks well worth following. Dawson City, fairly useful on a soft surface on the Flat, has shown he acts on good to firm and dead ground over hurdles. **M. H. Easterby**

DERRING VALLEY

6 b.g. Derrylin
Chalke Valley (Ragstone)

Derring Valley put the small, emerging Lambourn stable of Alan Jones on the map when he won the Grade 2 White Satin Novices' Hurdle at Liverpool in April. A 25/1-shot he won on merit by three lengths from Rocktor, making relentless progress to press the leaders two out (where the second favourite Smith's Cracker fell under pressure), gradually wearing down the leading trio of New Duds, Rocktor and Montagnard, and continuing to stay on strongly after going in front approaching the last. It was a very useful performance, especially for one having only his second run over hurdles. It was also that of a thorough stayer, for the event was run over twenty-five

❚ Derring Valley (right)
stays on too strongly for Rocktor

furlongs on dead ground. When Derring Valley went next for a well-contested novice handicap at Ayr run over three furlongs less on a firm surface, he was never able to land a blow, though a respectable ninth, behind Jodami. Forcing tactics on soft going had previously brought Derring Valley a win in a two-mile National Hunt Flat race at Uttoxeter on the first of three starts in that type of event—at odds of 50/1.

With other winners Kings Wild (four races), Hawksworth Lad and Thamesdown Tootsie (one each) the last season was one of definite progress for the stable. Derring Valley should lead the way further forward in 1991/2. Whether he'll make the top grade of staying hurdlers is doubtful but we fancy him strongly to do well in long-distance handicaps. While it would be asking too much for a repeat of his winning SP's, he should pay to follow. **A. P. Jones**

FISHKI | 5 b.m. Niniski
Ladyfish (Pampapaul)

Former jockey Michael Hammond enjoyed a tremendous first season as a trainer, sending out thirty-one winners and collecting around £100,000 in win and place money. Of the inmates at Tupgill Park Stables, Middleham, Fishki is one of the more interesting, and appeals as one to follow in handicap hurdles over two and a half miles-plus when the ground is testing. A modest middle-distance performer on the Flat, Fishki won two of her four starts in her first season hurdling—a novice event at Ayr in November and a handicap on the same course in March, both run on soft ground. In the latter she accounted for a field of experienced horses in comfortable fashion, leading from the fourth and drawing clear in the straight to beat Landski six lengths. Though Fishki clearly relishes the mud, she showed on her final start that she's capable of form on a firm surface. On that start, in a competitive novice handicap at Ayr again, she made the running and stuck on most gamely when joined by impressive winner Jodami four out, and was run out of a place only in the closing stages, eventually finishing seventh, beaten around thirteen lengths. Given a return to soft ground, we feel sure Fishki will win races. **M. D. Hammond**

GLENBROOK D'OR | 7 b.g. Le Coq d'Or
Wedderburn (Royalty)

In its review of the 1989 Irish point-to-point season *Formcard* described dual winner Glenbrook d'Or as 'very promising' and 'a tough, staying type who should have good chasing prospects'. Hardly surprising, then, that the horse should fetch as much as 28,000 guineas at the Doncaster Spring Sales that year. Unfortunately Glenbrook d'Or has been seen out only twice since, but he showed enough on his reappearance run in March to suggest that he could yet fulfil his early promise. A 33/1-shot for a two-and-a-half-mile maiden hurdle at Newbury, Glenbrook d'Or very much caught the eye in finishing second of twenty behind Everaldo, making up a lot of ground in the straight to get to within three lengths of the winner. Improvement was to be expected from the sturdy Glenbrook d'Or, who'd looked on the backward side, so it was disappointing to see him finish well down the field in the White Satin Novices' Hurdle at Liverpool less than two weeks later. It's possible that he hadn't fully recovered from his exertions at Newbury, and we think he's well worth another chance. Though his long-term future lies in steeplechases, he's certainly capable of winning races at two and a half miles and more over hurdles. **A. J. Wilson**

GOLD CAP (FR)
6 ch.g. Noir Et Or
Alkmaar (USA) (Verbatim (USA))

While such as Bokaro, Chatam, Reve de Valse, Rolling Ball and Sabin du Loir were highly successful in 1990/1 another ex-French horse, Gold Cap, failed to win and remains a novice both over hurdles and fences. We'll be very disappointed if he doesn't put matters right this season. Gold Cap showed plenty of ability in two of his three starts over fences for Charlie Brooks's stable, while he also ran with some promise in a handicap hurdle at Ascot on his only outing for his present trainer. Gold Cap, who'd acquitted himself well against stable-companion Espy in the Fairlawne Chase at Windsor, was sent off one of the favourites for Cheltenham's National Hunt Chase, run over four miles. His stamina unproven, Gold Cap was travelling well enough when falling three out to suggest that he'd have gone very close to beating Smooth Escort had he completed. Placed twice at around two and a half miles on heavy ground in France in the first half of last season, Gold Cap was raced only at three miles in Britain apart from at Cheltenham, on ground ranging from firm at Ascot to good to soft at Windsor. **P. J. Hobbs**

GREEK FLUTTER
6 b.g. Beldale Flutter (USA)
Greek Blessing (So Blessed)

We waited most of last season for Greek Flutter to run on a sound surface: he's suited by it on the Flat, in which sphere he's had some success at up to a mile and a half. When the day came, in a well-contested, good-class novice hurdle over two and a half miles at Ascot in April, he showed improved form though having to settle for third place behind Springaleak and Tim Soldier, beaten five lengths and four after chasing the leader Springaleak up the straight. He didn't race again. In four previous starts Greek Flutter was never out of the frame in two-mile novice hurdles in the North, and the start before Ascot he won from Robert Dear in testing conditions at Wetherby, lasting the race out better than the second. It will be interesting to see how Greek Flutter turns out in handicap hurdles—what his optimum distance will be, two miles or two and a half, and by how much a sound surface suits him best. What's clear is that he possesses a turn of foot and should do well. **J. G. FitzGerald**

HAITHAM | 4 b.c. Wassl
Balqis (USA) (Advocator)

Haitham's performances over long distances on the Flat in 1991—he finished second in the Ascot Stakes and won the Goodwood Stakes—suggest strongly that he'll improve significantly when returned to further than two miles over hurdles. Two and a half miles was the longest distance Haitham tackled in his first season over hurdles, and on that occasion he failed to do himself justice on softish ground. A winner over two-and-a-quarter miles on good ground at Fontwell on his debut, Haitham ran well on firm ground on his last two starts, though he was found wanting for finishing speed against Eurolink The Lad at Fontwell and Belafonte at Haydock. Haitham will be a different proposition back at two and a half miles, given suitable ground conditions, and he's one to follow in handicap hurdles. **R. Akehurst**

IAMA ZULU | 6 ch.g. Son of Shaka
Quick Sort (Henry The Seventh)

To look at him, Iama Zulu is the sort of whom trainers are fond of saying 'anything he wins before he goes chasing will be a bonus'. He's a rangy gelding with lots of physical scope; one, indeed, whom we have always thought would make more of a mark as a chaser than a hurdler. Iama Zulu, a modest winner over hurdles, has had one run over fences to date. It came on his last outing in 1990/1 in an interesting little handicap at Wincanton on Boxing Day, where he shaped with some promise in finishing third to Came Down, running on quite well to be beaten only four lengths after being held up until four out, jumping soundly. Iama Zulu will be resuming his chasing career this season, and shouldn't be difficult to place, either in minor handicaps or novice events at around two miles (he races keenly and barely stays two and a half). He has shown he acts on firm and dead going. **P. J. Hobbs**

JODAMI | 6 b.g. Crash Course
Masterstown Lucy (Bargello)

The small string of jumpers trained by Peter Beaumont at Brandsby, just outside York, enjoyed a fine season in 1990/1 with twelve wins, worth close on £50,000. The stable's most valuable success came from twelve-year-old J-J-Henry in the John Hughes Memorial Trophy at Liverpool. However, the first-season hurdler Jodami, winner of a National Hunt Flat race in 1989/90, wasn't far behind him in first-place money and won on five of his six starts in novice events, culminating in an impressive twelve-length victory in a competitive sixteen-runner handicap at Ayr in April. Jodami turned that race, the Scottish Farm Dairy Foods Hurdle, into a procession after taking the lead two out and he ran on strongly until eased a couple of lengths near the finish. That very useful performance stamped the six-year-old as a progressive young hurdler likely to go on to further success over timber in 1991/2. However, we understand that he is to be sent over fences in the coming season. Not that that dampens our enthusiasm in

| Scottish Farm Dairy Foods Novices' Handicap Hurdle, Ayr—
| Jodami is an impressive winner

recommending him as a horse to follow. Far from it. He's a grand type of animal and we can think of few better chasing prospects. It would come as no surprise if Jodami proved as successful in his first season over fences as he was in his first over hurdles. Although he won over two miles on his hurdling debut, Jodami was beaten for finishing speed by Robert Dear over the minimum trip at Wetherby next time and was subsequently campaigned over longer distances. The way he finished at Ayr suggests that he'll have little difficulty in staying further than two and three quarter miles. The going was good to firm that day and he won on soft on his fourth start. He's most definitely one to keep on the right side in 1991/2. **P. Beaumont**

KINGS FOUNTAIN

| 8 br.g. Royal Fountain
| K-King (Fury Royal)

When trainer Kim Bailey said in a *Timeform Interview* published late in January that as far as he was concerned the world was Kings Fountain's oyster, readers could have been excused for thinking that he'd taken leave of his senses. At the time Kings Fountain had failed to win from three starts in poor chasing company and looked to have problems with his jumping. Naturally they would think differently now, for Kings Fountain won all but one of his remaining six starts and ended up as one of the most promising novice chasers around! For our part, we were as much taken by surprise by Kings Fountain's huge improvement as the next man. However, a clear-cut success under a seemingly prohibitive burden in a novice handicap chase at Bangor in April certainly made us sit up and take notice. The transformation in Kings Fountain's form came alongside a marked improvement in his jumping and in his ability under faster conditions to see out two and a half miles. Kings Fountain's chief victim at Bangor, Sillian, had to play

14

**Kings Fountain
holds off Mighty Falcon and Givus A Buck
at Ascot**

second fiddle again when the pair lined up for a well-contested novice chase at Worcester in May. Making the running as usual, Kings Fountain soon had his opponents strung out, was in little trouble in the closing stages and eventually passed the post fifteen lengths and more to the good. That was Kings Fountain's final run of the season. Given his rate of progress it surely won't be long before he goes for bigger prizes. We're confident that he'll continue to justify his trainer's high opinion of him (he's seen as an embryo National horse) by making his mark in such company. At present, he seems well suited by forcing the pace over two and a half miles on firmish going. **K. C. Bailey**

LAUNDRYMAN ▮ 8 b.g. Celtic Cone
Lovely Laura (Lauso)

Laundryman looks the type to have on your side in handicap chases at up to two and a half miles. Stan Mellor's charge graduated from a poor novice hurdler into a promising chaser in 1990/1, winning five races on the trot. Though his form in those contests didn't amount to a great deal, he would surely have run to a much higher figure had he completed in a well-contested novice event at Sandown on his penultimate start. In that race, he was still on the bridle in second

**| Laundryman is one to follow
| in handicap chases**

place when departing at the fourth last, leaving the good novices Golden Celtic and Esha Ness to fight out the finish. Laundryman was below his best in the Golden Eagle Novices' Chase at Ascot next time, running a lack-lustre race until falling two out. We're prepared to forgive that effort, as he left the impression he was feeling the effects of his long season and probably the good to firm going—all his wins were achieved with give in the ground. Laundryman starts the season on a very favourable handicap mark. An ideal race to go for with him would be the two-and-a-half-mile H & T Walker Gold Cup, a limited handicap for second-season chasers, at Ascot in November. **S. Mellor**

MACARTHUR **| 6 b.g. Ardross
| Polly Peachum (Singing Strand)**

The end-of-term comment on Macarthur in 1989/90 read 'jumps hurdles well and should make a chaser'. We hope the latest one, 'a useful chaser in the making', works out just as well. Macarthur certainly looks to be going the right way: he won three of his seven races in his first season over fences in 1990/1 and finished in the frame on all his others. His biggest success, following those in ordinary novice events at Newcastle (a handicap) and Sedgefield, came in the quite valuable two-and-a-half-mile amateur riders novice handicap at Liverpool on Grand National day. One of three co-favourites in a field of ten, Macarthur once again impressed with his jumping. Racing in a

Macarthur (right) just gets the better of William Anthony at Liverpool

clear second for most of the way, he jumped into the lead four out, and though hard pressed by William Anthony, he maintained a narrow advantage until a typically efficient jump at the last enabled him finally to get the upper hand. Macarthur had one and a half lengths to spare over William Anthony at the post, the pair twenty lengths clear. Macarthur, who is unlikely to stay beyond two and a half miles, looks to have plenty more improvement in him, and will pay his way in 1991/2. He's yet to race on heavy going but has shown he acts on any other. **M. W. Easterby**

MONUMENTAL LAD

8 ro.g. Jellaby
Monumental Moment (St Paddy)

Having taken a much higher view of Monumental Lad's recent performances over fences than the official handicapper, we'll be disappointed if he fails to take full advantage of his present mark. Monumental Lad developed into quite a useful novice last season and won at Worcester and Huntingdon, giving an impressive performance under top weight in a conditional jockeys handicap on the latter course. Always going smoothly, jumping very well, Monumental Lad took up the running five from home and steadily drew clear to score by twenty lengths from Hope End. Not surprisingly Monumental Lad was no match for Remittance Man in his two subsequent races, but he acquitted himself well. He finished runner-up in the Galloway Braes Novices' Chase at Kempton and seventh in the Waterford Castle Arkle

Trophy at Cheltenham. He's likely to have his sights lowered considerably in the coming season. A big, strong, plain gelding, Monumental Lad stays two and a half miles and acts on soft going. **Mrs H. Parrott**

MORLEY STREET
7 ch.g. Deep Run
High Board (High Line)

Morley Street is included not because he's the Champion Hurdler but because of his marked superiority to the other contenders last season, plus his potential for improvement should he be tested more strenuously this. Morley Street's superiority was most clearly demonstrated in the Sandeman Aintree Hurdle on his final start, when he quadrupled his advantage over Nomadic Way. Morley Street had struck the front a shade too soon at Cheltenham to show to best advantage—he'd been travelling so well with the leaders at the second last that he left Jimmy Frost little option except to go on—and he'd idled in front as is his wont. At Liverpool the horse was very impressive, spreadeagling as strong a field of hurdlers as was assembled all season. He cantered all over Nomadic Way up the straight, showed ahead approaching the last and quickened away after putting in a good jump. Behind Nomadic Way, who finished a six-length second, came the good stayer Run For Free and Champion Hurdle runners Bradbury Star, Mole Board, The Illiad and Jinxy Jack, with Cloughtaney and another Champion Hurdle contender, Fidway, bringing up the rear.

At the time of writing Morley Street has begun warming up for the new season by running in very useful company on the Flat. He was very much in need of the outing when he finished fourth in the Lonsdale Stakes at the York Ebor meeting after his summer break. Plans are for him to have at least one other race on the Flat, then an attempt at a repeat win in the Breeders' Cup Steeplechase in the USA

I Morley Street leads the field in the Breeders' Cup Chase

in the autumn before resuming his hurdling career. The Champion Hurdle and the Aintree Hurdle are at the top of the agenda; it's not envisaged that he'll return to jumping British fences (at which he showed some aptitude before becoming disappointing in 1990/1) before 1992/3 at the earliest. The rangy Morley Street acts on any going. His turn of foot and jumping ability will continue to make him a very difficult horse to beat. **G. B. Balding**

MR MONDAY | 5 b.g. Over The River (FR)
Miss Monday (Master Owen)

Here's an interesting long-term prospect, a darker horse than any of the other forty-nine. On the face of it, Mr Monday has little to recommend him, having run just once, unquoted and sixth of seventeen in a novice hurdle at Wetherby in May. That's not the whole story, though. It would have been no surprise if Mr Monday, an unfurnished gelding, on the backward side and from the typically patient stable of Arthur Stephenson, had shown nothing at all in the circumstances. But show something he did, staying on nicely under tender handling having jumped deliberately and left himself with plenty to do. For Mr Monday to be beaten only about thirty lengths by the fair performer Nessfield was encouraging, particularly as he left the impression that a good deal better was to come when he develops physically and gains more experience.

There's a fair amount of encouragement to be derived from Mr Monday's breeding as well. While his dam was unraced and has produced little of consequence from three previous foals, she's more notable as a sister of the high-class hurdler Master Monday, winner of the Sweeps Hurdle and the Erin Foods Champion Hurdle in 1976/7. Furthermore, Mr Monday's sire, Over The River, has been a notable success at stud, particularly as a sire of chasers. We imagine it won't be long before Mr Monday goes over fences himself, but, in the meantime, we'll be disappointed if he doesn't win novice hurdles at the lesser tracks. **W. A. Stephenson**

MUSE | 4 ch.g. High Line
Thoughtful (Northfields (USA))

Muse is very much one to look out for in novice hurdles in 1991/2, especially when given the opportunity to tackle distances beyond two miles. He has been placed on each of his three starts, running moderately at Wincanton second time up but shaping with plenty of promise over the much stiffer courses at Cheltenham and Newbury. At Cheltenham Muse kept on well to finish ten lengths second to the smart Hopscotch, ahead of four other winning hurdlers, in the Food Brokers Finesse Hurdle. And at Newbury he went down by three lengths to Pashto, the pair clear of the remainder. Muse's jumping still leaves something to be desired, but it will improve as he gains experience.

Muse was bought out of Major Hern's stable for 22,000 guineas at the Newmarket Autumn Sales after winning twice at a mile and a half. He showed better form when returned to the Flat in March, being successful over the same trip and then coming an excellent third in the two-mile Queen's Prize at Kempton. Muse, who probably acts on any going on the Flat, raced on good to soft ground at Wincanton and good at Cheltenham and Newbury. **D. R. C. Elsworth**

MUTARE |
6 b.g. Boreen (FR)
Slave Trade (African Sky)

Mutare joined his present stable after winning all three of his starts over hurdles in Ireland last season, and continued to show useful form. Fifth in the Top Rank Christmas Hurdle at Kempton, where he was found wanting for finishing speed, Mutare then ran well when returned to two and a half miles, in the Bishops Cleeve Hurdle at Cheltenham. Mutare, who usually helps force the pace, set a good gallop at Cheltenham, and going to the last he'd shaken off all bar Crystal Spirit. Though keeping on gamely under pressure, he found Crystal Spirit just too strong for him up the hill. On his only subsequent start Mutare appeared not to stay in the twenty-five-furlong BonusPrint Stayers' Hurdle at Cheltenham, but it transpired that he'd had an interrupted preparation and it's possible that he was short of peak fitness. Mutare had run well at three miles in his first season over hurdles, and his trainer is of the opinion that he's a top-class three-mile chaser in the making. The well-made Mutare certainly looks the type who'll be seen to even better advantage over fences, and he's sure to win races in novice company. He acts on heavy going and has yet to race on ground firmer than good. **N. J. Henderson**

| Useful hurdler Mutare
| will be seen to even better advantage over fences

NEW YORK |
RAINBOW |
6 br.g. Good Thyne (USA)
Alice Starr (Windjammer (USA))

New York Rainbow, successful on the second of his two starts in National Hunt Flat races in Ireland in 1989/90, was placed in all three of his races over hurdles last season, novice events at Kempton, Ascot and Windsor. His best performance was at Ascot in January when a clear one and a half lengths second to Charlton Yeoman in the £4,000 Hairy Mary Novices' Hurdle. Held up initially, New York Rainbow had to be pushed along to improve his position approaching the home turn and then lacked the pace to get on terms with the winner, giving the strong impression that a distance longer than two miles will suit him. Nevertheless, a repetition of that form would be good enough to win most run-of-the-mill novice hurdles over the minimum trip, and we'll be surprised if he doesn't win a race or two over timber before going over fences. New York Rainbow is very much a chasing sort on looks and we expect his attentions will fairly shortly be turned in that direction. His three races over hurdles have been on dead going. **N. J. Henderson**

OBIE'S TRAIN
5 ch.g. Buckskin (FR)
Whisper Moon (Chinatown)

This latest of the largely-successful line of 'Train' horses handled by Jenny Pitman for Mr Oberstein is a promising successor to the likes of Midnight Train, The A Train and so on. Obie's Train is a well-grown individual who just lacks experience at present. It showed in his last race in 1990/1 when he came fourth of twenty-one finishers behind Ben Adhem in a novice hurdle at Newbury in March. He took a good hold, waited with, and after he'd moved towards the leaders entering the home straight he made mistakes at the last two flights, but for which he'd have finished closer to the winner than the twenty or so lengths he was eventually beaten. That was only the third race of Obie's Train's career. He'd shown up on his hurdling debut in the novice event at Ascot in which New York Rainbow finished second; before that, in late-December, he'd finished second of twenty-four in a National Hunt Flat race at Warwick.

The run at Newbury will have brought Obie's Train on a ton. He shouldn't be long in getting off the mark in novice hurdle company this season once he's fit, and he'll go on from there. Obie's Train cost IR 16,000 guineas as a three-year-old at Tattersalls Derby Sale, the source of a number of Mrs Pitman's winners, notably Garrison Savannah. He's well bred, as you might guess. His dam, who's produced a winning hurdler by Pauper, is a half-sister to the good hunter chaser Edenspring and to Emperor's Gift, the dam of the late, lamented Mrs Muck. The third dam bred the smart staying chaser High Ken. Looking at the pedigree, there seems little doubt that as long as he settles Obie's Train will stay, and be suited by, further than the two miles he has thus far tackled. **Mrs J. Pitman**

O'REILLY
8 b.g. Certingo
Bohemian Girl (Pardao)

Following a few lean seasons the Stan Mellor stable, now relocated near Swindon, was back on song in 1990/1 sending out the winners of thirty-four races. O'Reilly, one of the yard's lesser lights, was responsible for two of those wins, and this progressive chaser looks sure to continue to make a worthwhile contribution.

A successful point-to-pointer in Ireland, O'Reilly got off the mark for Mellor in a novice chase at Sedgefield in January. Making most of the running, he jumped well in the main and stayed on strongly to beat Mowthorpe by five lengths. In a similar event at Plumpton later in the month, O'Reilly was ridden with restraint when beating Afaltoun by six lengths, challenging at the last and soon drawing clear. Though both races were over two miles, we would expect O'Reilly to be at least as effective over slightly longer trips. He wasn't fully wound up when tackling two and a half miles and three miles earlier in the season. O'Reilly, a rangy gelding, raced only on a soft surface in 1990/1. **S. Mellor**

PAPERWORK BOY
6 ch.g. Buckskin (FR)
Orinda Way (Deep Run)

The winner of National Hunt Flat races at Huntingdon in October and Hexham in November on his first two starts, Paperwork Boy showed more than enough on his only run over hurdles to suggest that he'll also be worth following in novice company. Having his first outing for four months, Paperwork Boy finished ten lengths second to No More Trix at Sedgefield in March, disputing the lead from four out until unable to quicken from the second last, being eased once his chance had gone. Paperwork Boy's jumping was none too fluent, but it will improve as he gains experience. A lengthy, good sort, with plenty of scope, Paperwork Boy's long-term future lies over fences, but there are plenty of races to be won with him over hurdles first. He'll stay beyond two and a half miles. **M. H. Easterby**

PARTY POLITICS
7 br.g. Politico (USA)
Spin Again (Royalty)

Watch out for Party Politics in good-class staying handicap chases. One of the leading novices in 1989/90 he developed into a very useful performer last season, winning handicaps at Newbury in October and December and the three-runner Warwick Premier Chase in January from five starts. He ran a fine race in defeat when going down by two lengths to Celtic Shot in the Edward Hanmer Memorial Chase, a limited handicap at Haydock on his second outing, receiving 16 lb from the winner, but he looked out of his depth when tackling the best chasers at level weights in the Tote Cheltenham Gold Cup in March, in which he was behind when pulled up four out. A big, rangy gelding, and still relatively young, Party Politics, who jumps well and races with plenty of zest, may well have further improvement in him and should have plenty of opportunities of a big pay day. He starts the season quite well treated considering his achievements in 1990/1 and strikes us as an ideal prospect for the Hennessy Cognac Gold Cup at Newbury in November. **N. A. Gaselee**

PLAT REAY

7 b.g. Uncle Pokey
Hejera (Cantab)

Plat Reay's stable is first and foremost a chasing stable. Almost all its inmates who aren't chasers already will be one day, and are given whatever time and assistance they need to develop. Plat Reay himself showed only a little over hurdles but, brought along steadily, really blossomed on his last two outings over fences in 1990/1 and looks a good find. He won both those races, novice events on dead ground over two miles at Towcester and two and a half at Uttoxeter, at the chief expense of a promising horse of Henderson's called Le Piccolage on the first occasion, and the more exposed Sweet City on the second. Plat Reay was impressive against Sweet City, confirming himself a sound jumper and very much a progressive sort. He was always moving well, held the lead from five out apart from a brief moment four out, and kept on strongly to win easily.

Plat Reay's dam, the once-raced Hejera, is a fairly close relative of the 1981 Gold Cup winner—she's by Little Owl's sire Cantab out of a half-sister to Little Owl's dam. She's also a half-sister to the useful chaser Marnik who got three miles well. Yet Plat Reay's stamina is uncertain. His brothers, the winning hurdler Men of Yorkshire and the novice hurdler Draw Poker, have shown more speed than stamina. He himself has yet to show he stays further than two and a half miles, and he gave the impression when tried over three immediately prior to Towcester—admittedly on very heavy going which might not have suited him—that he is not an out-and-out stayer. Furthermore, he takes a good hold, and the chances are at this stage that he'll prove best at distances short of three miles. Whatever his distance, Plat Reay looks like making up into a useful handicap chaser over the next few months. **Capt. T. A. Forster**

❚ **Party Politics in action at Newbury**

PRIME DISPLAY (USA)
5 ch.g. Golden Act (USA)
Great Display (FR) (Great Nephew)

A 15,500-guinea purchase off the Flat at the Newmarket Autumn Sales, Prime Display took some time to reach a similar standard over hurdles though he started off in fine style, winning a novice event at Leicester in January on his debut. He failed to find the anticipated improvement on his next three outings, looking one-paced when third in a twenty-five-furlong race on good to firm ground at Doncaster on the second of them. However, things began to look up again following a very easy win from inferior opponents at Lingfield in March, and later that month he put up his best performance when beating the favourite Maestro Paul by three and a half lengths in an eighteen-runner event over two and a half miles at Worcester. Giving weight all round, he made all and won in comfortable fashion, suggesting plenty more improvement was still to come. Prime Display has the makings of a useful handicapper, and should pay to follow over two and a half miles and more. He gave the impression at Doncaster that he was possibly unsuited by the firm surface, and his best form is with plenty of give in the ground. **O. Sherwood**

QUENTIN DURWOOD
5 gr.g. Mr Fluorocarbon
Donallan (No Mercy)

Last of ten finishers when favourite for the Polycell Hurdle at Chepstow and nearer last than first in a novice event at Ascot on his most recent starts, Quentin Durwood would seem to be a horse to treat with some caution. Yet we think he's well worth another chance to confirm the promise of his first two runs. Quentin Durwood floundered in the heavy ground at Chepstow, and while he might not have been suited by the firm going at Ascot it's more likely that he found the distance of two and a half miles beyond him. Quentin Durwood had won his two previous races, both of them over two miles, in good style, sprinting fifteen lengths clear in the closing stages at Huntingdon and again showing a turn of foot when landing the odds by ten lengths at Stratford. The ground was good to soft on the former course, soft on the latter. Quentin Durwood is unlikely to be overburdened in handicaps as a result of his defeats, and he'll win races when conditions are in his favour. **Mrs J. Pitman**

REMITTANCE MAN
7 b.g. Prince Regent (FR)
Mittens (Run The Gantlet (USA))

Very few novice chasers have impressed as much with the speed, confidence and style of their jumping as Remittance Man did in the most recent season. Anaglogs Daughter in 1979/80 and Pendil in 1971/2 are two that spring to mind as making similar light of jumping fences as novices. Following success in the Arkle Challenge Trophy at the Cheltenham Festival meeting, the last two developed into

**Remittance Man
and Richard Dunwoody**

top-class chasers in their following season over fences; and Remittance Man, winner of the latest running of the Arkle, is odds on to do the same. Make no mistake, he has a major role to play in the very best company, and we'll go so far as to say that he could well eventually rank alongside some of the very best chasers of recent years.

The Arkle was the last of Remittance Man's six races in his first season over fences and maintained his unbeaten record over the larger obstacles, following earlier successes at Leicester, Newbury, Ascot and Kempton (two). Except for the Arkle and the race at Leicester which were over two miles, Remittance Man's races over fences have been over two and a half miles. If anything, he is likely to be even more effective at distances around three miles. As a hurdler he ran up to his best when second to Miinnehoma in the twenty-five-furlong Philip Cornes Saddle Of Gold Final at Newbury. The three-mile King George VI Rank Chase at Kempton on Boxing Day is likely to be Remittance Man's principal objective in the first half of the season. Desert Orchid has dominated the King George in recent years but by the next running Remittance Man, provided all goes well with him, could take centre stage. His prospects for the Gold Cup look quite bright as well, though his ability to last out the three-and-a-quarter-mile trip will be easier to judge at a later date. Remittance Man has yet to race on extremes of going but acts on any other. We look forward with relish to seeing him return to action. **N. J. Henderson**

RHODES | 4 ch.g. Pharly (FR)
Beacon Hill (Bustino)

Rhodes was a 16,000-guinea bargain-buy out of Major Hern's stable at the Newmarket Autumn Sales in 1990. At the time, there was little about him to suggest that he was from one of the best families in the Stud Book, out of a sister to Nashwan's dam Height of Fashion: he was just a modest staying maiden. Sent hurdling during the winter, he began showing form straight away though his jumping left something to be desired, and on the last of four outings he got off the mark in a two-mile novice handicap at Nottingham in January. Since then Rhodes has put in another stint on the Flat and has shown significantly improved form in long-distance handicaps, winning in excellent style at Folkestone and Bath. Given that Rhodes has shown such improvement, that his jumping seems bound to get better with experience and that he is likely to prove suited by further than two miles, he should be worth following in handicap hurdles. **J. Akehurst**

▌ Romany King

ROMANY ▌
KING

**7 br.g. Crash Course
Winsome Lady (Tarqogan)**

This progressive chaser, who won two handicaps at both Chepstow and Warwick and was placed on his other starts last season, is young enough to keep one step ahead of the handicapper for quite a while yet. He's developing into a useful performer at around two and a half miles. Though he was far from disgraced on top-of-the-ground when third to John O'Dee in the Peregrine Handicap Chase at Ascot in April on his final start, Romany King, we are sure, will ultimately prove better with some give—his four successes during the season were gained on dead or soft going. At Ascot Romany King was held up, as usual, but unlike in his earlier races in which he travelled smoothly, he needed to be niggled along from an early stage to keep in touch. He made rapid headway from four out to join issue at the second last, but the effort of getting there so quickly took its toll and he found no extra approaching the last.

Romany King has now won eight of his twenty-two races over jumps in a three-season career and has failed to complete the course only once—when brought down. He's a very sound jumper, capable of giving a good account of himself in good-class handicaps (as he showed when second to Foyle Fisherman in the valuable Mildmay Of Flete Challenge Cup at the Cheltenham Festival) as well as when conceding weight in smaller events. **G. B. Balding**

RONANS BIRTHDAY | 9 b.g. Furry Glen
Mountain Sedge (Goldhill)

Not too many nine-year-olds make our Fifty To Follow but we don't hesitate in putting forward Ronans Birthday. With just a point-to-point success under his belt prior to last season, he made up for lost time around the turn of the year, winning handicap chases at Bangor (a novice event), Wincanton (a conditional jockeys race) and Windsor. On the last-named course in January he was made favourite to beat quite a competitive field and did so in the style of a fast-improving horse, by six lengths from Tom Bir. He failed to turn out again due to a training set-back, which was frustrating since he was in such good form, but he's reportedly fully fit again and will be in action in 1991/2. Ronans Birthday stays twenty-five furlongs, but has a useful turn of foot and is effective at two and a half miles, making him easier to place. Raced once on heavy ground and yet to race on very firm, he acts on any other. Ronans Birthday should again pay his way for trainer Hobbs who took him over from Mrs Oliver after five starts in 1990/1. The horse's two wins from two starts for the stable took Hobbs's final total for the season to an excellent thirty-three. **P. J. Hobbs**

ROSS VENTURE | 6 b.g. Monksfield
Fitz's Buck (Master Buck)

Although Ross Venture had an excellent first season over the sticks it's doubtful that we've seen the best of him yet, especially over fences. After impressively winning novice hurdles at Uttoxeter in October and Wolverhampton in November, he was beaten only once in four novice chases, scoring at Market Rasen (in an amateur riders event) in April and Hereford and Warwick (in a handicap) in May. His best performance over fences came on the last-named course where he justified favouritism by ten lengths from Cleaning Up with the remainder well strung out. Ross Venture, a free galloper, made all the running at Warwick, as he had in nearly all of his races. He's unlikely to stay beyond two and a half miles for the time being. Ross Venture ran moderately when tried on soft ground in the middle of his campaign, and seems well suited by a sound surface. Ross Venture has plenty of time on his side and looks an interesting prospect for handicap chases given the right ground. **J. A. C. Edwards**

ROYAL ASTRONAUT (USA)
7 ch.g. Grey Dawn II
Short Stanza (USA) (Verbatim (USA))

Here's one to have on your side in long-distance handicap hurdles when there's plenty of give in the ground. Royal Astronaut is useful in that company. Having looked short of peak fitness on his first two starts last season, he came good in a twenty-seven-runner qualifier of the Coral Golden Hurdle on softish going at Nottingham in January, winning in good style by six lengths from Mossgara. Having been held up, Royal Astronaut made steady headway in the back straight, moved through to join the leader after three out, led at the next and began to draw clear halfway up the run-in. The ground wasn't so testing for Royal Astronaut's only subsequent race, the Coral Golden Hurdle Final at Cheltenham in March. In the circumstances he was far from disgraced in coming around eight lengths seventh of the twenty-three finishers behind Danny Connors, and had conditions been more testing there's every chance he'd have figured in the finish. Granted plenty of give in the ground and provided all goes well with him, Royal Astronaut should give a better account of himself in the next Coral Golden Hurdle Final. Whatever his fate at Cheltenham he seems sure to win more races when conditions are in his favour. **R. Akehurst**

SHANNON GLEN
5 b.g. Furry Glen
Shannon Ville (Deep Run)

Here's a good prospect, by the sire of Gold Cup runner-up Toby Tobias out of a Deep Run mare who's a sister to Bee Sting, a smart novice hurdler in 1980/1. Shannon Ville herself won a National Hunt Flat race, a two-mile maiden hurdle and a two-and-a-quarter-mile novice chase in Ireland, and is also out of the dam of the Gold Cup winner Glencaraig Lady and the great-grandam of Maid of Money and Ten of Spades. Until running poorly at Ayr on his final outing when racing on a firm surface for the first time, Shannon Glen lived up to his breeding, improving steadily into a leading novice in his first season over hurdles. He clearly benefited from a step up in distance when running out an impressive winner of the two-and-a-half mile Mumm Prize Novices' Hurdle at Liverpool on his penultimate start. Having taken closer order as the tempo increased leaving the back straight, Shannon Glen moved into the lead approaching two out and stayed on strongly for an eight-length success over Crystal Spirit. Although Crystal Spirit failed to run up to the form he'd shown when winning the Sun Alliance Novices' Hurdle at Cheltenham on his previous start, Shannon Glen still put up a very useful performance. A lengthy, chasing type with plenty of scope, Shannon Glen is still open to improvement over hurdles, but he has the build to suggest that he won't come fully into his own until sent chasing. Our guess is that that will be sooner rather than later, particularly as the official handicapper appears to have taken a high view of his form. And unless appearances are very deceptive Shannon Glen should take high rank among the staying novice chasers in 1991/2, in which his obvious long-term objective would be the Sun Alliance Novices' Chase at the Cheltenham Festival Meeting. **Mrs J. Pitman**

TARDA | 4 ch.f. Absalom
Ixia (I Say)

Tarda and her half-sister Corn Lily have ended up in the same stable again after taking similar routes during their careers—via Pritchard-Gordon, Nigel Tinkler and the sale-ring. Mrs Reveley was persuaded to speculate 11,000 guineas on Tarda at the Doncaster March Sales for other reasons, apparently, besides the fact that she had Corn Lily—the filly was also a half-sister to a good servant of the stable in the staying chaser Trailing Rose, she looked as though she'd jump fences in time, she also had potential as a broodmare. There *was* a clear element of speculation about the purchase, for Tarda had lost her form on her last two outings on the Flat as a three-year-old and her one run over jumps had resulted in only fourth place in a juvenile selling hurdle at Worcester in September. However, Tarda's form on the Flat during the summer has been a revelation—she's won handicaps at Ripon over a mile and over nine furlongs and is better than ever—and, as with several other horses in this selection, we're hoping that her improvement will be reflected in her jumping form. **Mrs G. R. Reveley**

TREFELYN CONE | 7 ch.m. Celtic Cone
Trefelyn Heather (Arctic Chevalier)

The genuine and versatile Trefelyn Cone began last season with an impressive thirty-length win in a mares novice chase at Leicester, and ended it by capturing the valuable Martell Handicap Hurdle at Liverpool. Her jumping had let her down in two races over fences in between, hence the return to hurdling. Trefelyn Cone got no further than the first on her second start over fences, and next time out she jumped left and made some mistakes prior to falling two out in a mares novice handicap at Haydock. Trefelyn Cone, who was conceding a lot of weight all round, would probably have finished a good second to Mulloch Brae at Haydock had she completed, and we've rated her accordingly. That is to say that we regard her chasing form as being on a par with her hurdling form. As Trefelyn Cone's official mark over fences is 16 lb lower than that over hurdles she'll surely do well in handicap chases, provided her jumping problems are sorted out. Trefelyn Cone, a plain, sparely-made mare, will stay at least three

Trefelyn Cone (right)
makes a successful return
to hurdling

miles. Yet to race on very soft ground, she acts on any other. **M. C. Pipe**

UNSHAKEABLE | 5 b.g. Oats
Another Breeze (Deep Run)

Unshakeable is the first foal of Another Breeze, a very useful staying chaser in the early 'eighties when trained, like Unshakeable, by Nick Gaselee. Another Breeze gained her most important successes at Ascot, in the Pearce Duff Novices' Handicap Chase and the Green Highlander Handicap Chase, in the latter trouncing Tracys Special, Approaching and Corbiere among others. On the same course in April Unshakeable got off the mark over hurdles at the third attempt, in a two-and-a-half-mile novice event run on soft ground. Taking up the running three out, he quickened into the straight and needed only to be pushed along to score by ten lengths and five from previous winners Driving Force and Catchapenny, whom he met at level weights. Kept to hurdling Unshakeable would have a bright future in staying handicaps, but it's probable that he'll have his attentions turned to chasing this season. A strong, lengthy, good sort, he looks sure to make his mark in novice company. **N. A. Gaselee**

VICOMPT DE VALMONT | 6 b.g. Beau Charmeur (FR)
Wish Again (Three Wishes)

Bought for 40,000 guineas in Ireland as a four-year-old, Vicompt de Valmont has so far recouped only £259.60 of his purchase price, through a third placing in a National Hunt Flat race at Doncaster in January on his debut. Unless we're very much mistaken he'll pick up a great deal more than that in the coming season, for he shaped most encouragingly in novice hurdles at Towcester and Ascot and is sure to win races in similar company. Vicompt de Valmont put up the better performance when sixth of seventeen behind Springaleak in a quite well-contested event on the latter course, not being knocked about once his chance had gone having travelled well for a long way. That race was over two and a half miles, and Vicompt de Valmont is likely to need at least that distance to be seen to best advantage. A brother to the useful hurdler/chaser Willsford, winner of the Midlands Grand National, the leggy Vicompt de Valmont is out of an unraced half-sister to the fairly useful chaser Sandy Sprite, runner-up in the Welsh Grand National in 1971. **N. J. Henderson**

WELSHMAN | 5 ch.g. Final Straw
Joie de Galles (Welsh Pageant)

There'll be a welcome in the hillsides for Welshman if he fulfils our hopes for him. Our interest in him stems from the fact that he is an honest individual, by no means badly handicapped at present, and one from whom further improvement could be forthcoming. Added to that, he's likely to be campaigned realistically around the minor tracks, for the time being at least, as in the latest season. Welshman had only two wins to show from eight runs last term, but that was no disgrace all things considered. His first three runs were over two miles—a trip clearly short of his best as it transpired; he fell once when in with every chance of winning; and he was out of his depth once. That leaves three performances of consequence, covering his two wins when forcing the pace at around two and a half miles with plenty of give in the ground at Hereford in December and Chepstow in March, and a second placing to the well-treated Southover Lad over twenty-one furlongs on good going at Ludlow later in March. In truth, conditions at Ludlow scarcely made for a sufficient test of stamina for Welshman, but he acquitted himself as well as could be expected. Since then, Welshman has performed with credit over long distances on the Flat, making all on one occasion at Nottingham. We're very hopeful that Welshman will resume winning ways over hurdles when tried at around three miles. **M. Blanshard**

WONDER MAN (FR) | 6 ch.g. The Wonder (FR)
Juvenilia (FR) (Kashmir II)

The very smart hurdler Wonder Man has already been schooled over fences and is likely to be seen in action in novice chases in the second half of the season. A tall, lengthy individual, very much the type to make a chaser, he could well become a leading contender for the Waterford Castle Arkle Trophy at Cheltenham in March.

Before embarking on his chasing career Wonder Man is to have a crack at Kempton's Top Rank Christmas Hurdle, aiming to complete a hat-trick of victories at this particular meeting. The winner of the last two runnings of the Royal Garden Hotel Handicap Hurdle there, Wonder Man is sure to face a much stiffer test in the Christmas Hurdle, but it will take a very good hurdler to beat him. Wonder Man is a horse with a fine turn of foot, and he used it to good effect when

**HSS Hire Shops Hurdle, Ascot—
Wonder Man quickens clear**

beating Voyage Sans Retour by four lengths in the Welsh Champion Hurdle at Chepstow in April. But for a mistake at the last he'd have won even more decisively. Wonder Man, who acts on good to firm and soft going, is unlikely to be called upon to tackle distances beyond two miles; if he should be we wouldn't expect him to produce his best. **Mrs J. Pitman**

YOUNG BENZ

**7 ch.g. Young Generation
Cavalier's Blush (King's Troop)**

Any argument about the top two-mile novice chaser of 1990/1 would have to include Young Benz, who gave a similar beating to good horses in the Perrier Jouet Novices' Chase at Liverpool to that given by most people's number-one choice, Remittance Man, in the Arkle at Cheltenham. The Perrier Jouet attracted a very strong field. Remittance Man was missing but the second, third and fourth in the Arkle, Uncle Ernie (11-10), Redundant Pal (11-3) and Devil's Valley (11-3), took their chance, along with Aldino (11-10), Last 'o' The Bunch (11-7), Black Amber, High Knowl, My Young Man, Naatell and Young Benz (all 11-3). At the weights Young Benz came out easily best in a strongly-run race, winning by a long-looking twelve lengths and three from Uncle Ernie and Last 'o' The Bunch. Going to three out Young Benz was moving easiest, the race seeming to lie between him, Last 'o' The Bunch and Uncle Ernie by that stage, but he made a mistake at the fence. For a while after that the prize looked certain to go Uncle Ernie's way, until Young Benz staged a tremendous recovery and passed him as if he were stood still between the last two. Once over the last he drew further clear without undue effort.

The Perrier Jouet was Young Benz's sixth steeplechase. Smart over hurdles, he'd set off with three wins in ordinary company over fences but then successive falls at Ascot and Haydock persuaded connections to give the Arkle a miss and wait for Liverpool. After Liverpool he was sent to Ayr for the two-and-a-half-mile Edinburgh Woollen Mill's Future Champion Novices' Chase where, for the first time in his jumping career, he encountered a firm surface and a longer distance than two miles. He was never moving with the fluency he showed at Liverpool and finished sore on his near-fore in a modest third place behind High Knowl. The news is that Yong Benz is to come back into training this season. We doubt his being risked on anything firmer than good again (he acts well on soft) and don't expect to see him do much racing beyond two miles, though wouldn't rule out his staying two and a half. The chances are he'll prove best in strongly-run two-mile races (he has a fine turn of foot) and that he'll reach the top flight at that distance over fences. Best blinkered or visored on the Flat, he ran creditably on the only occasion he was blinkered over hurdles; he has yet to wear either aid over fences. **M. H. Easterby**

TRAINERS TIPS

Horses to follow from the top trainers

Instead of nominating a horse to follow from their own stable, which is the usual practice, we've asked leading trainers

NICKY HENDERSON
TOBY BALDING
JIMMY FITZGERALD
JENNY PITMAN
OLIVER SHERWOOD
KIM BAILEY
CHARLIE BROOKS
GORDON RICHARDS
MARTIN PIPE
DAVID ELSWORTH

to select a horse from another yard which they think will do well in the 1991/2 season. Read what they had to say overleaf.

CRYSTAL SPIRIT

trained by
Ian Balding

**4 b.g. Kris
Crown Treasure (USA)
(Graustark)**

selected by

Nicky Henderson & Toby Balding

After three seasons as assistant to Fred Winter Nicky Henderson, also a successful amateur rider, was granted a trainer's licence in July 1978. Since then he's sent out a stream of big-race winners, most notably See You Then, winner of the Champion Hurdle three times (1985-1987). Nicky's highest total of winners is 67, achieved in 1986/7. Nicky: **I adore this horse and I'll make no secret of the fact that, at one stage last season, I tried to buy him. Not surprisingly Ian told me pretty sharpish that he wasn't for sale. I've seen very few four-year-olds off the Flat with the physical scope he has. The performance he put up when beating Mutare, whom I train, in the Bishops Cleeve Hurdle at Cheltenham last January was outstanding.**

Toby Balding, who began training in 1957, at the age of twenty-one, is one of our longest holders of a licence. During the last thirty-four seasons he's enjoyed notable success on the Flat and under National Hunt rules, his best jumping tally being gained in 1988/9 with 59 successes. Toby has won the Grand National (Highland Wedding 1968, and Little Polveir 1989) and Champion Hurdle (Beech Road 1989, and Morley Street 1991). Toby: **My choice of Crystal Spirit has absolutely nothing to do with the fact that my brother Ian is his trainer. This is a lovely horse who did extremely well last season and who will, eventually, make up into a fine chaser. As the trainer of Morley Street I'm always on the look-out for possible dangers to him. I wouldn't in all honesty see Crystal Spirit being fast enough to trouble Morley Street over two miles but he might be a real threat in something like the Sandeman Hurdle at Aintree.**

DANNY CONNORS

trained by
Jonjo O'Neill

**7 b.g. Furry Glen
Steady Lady
(Lord Gayle (USA))**

selected by
Jimmy FitzGerald

Formerly a successful National Hunt jockey Jimmy FitzGerald has enjoyed a fine career since hanging up his boots. Beginning as a trainer in 1969 he's handled some fine horses, both on the Flat and over the sticks. The late Forgive N'Forget, probably his best horse over jumps to date, won the Cheltenham Gold Cup in 1985. Jimmy's best tally of winners was 73, in 1986/7. Jimmy: **Danny Connors is in some ways similar to my Gold Cup winner Forgive N'Forgive at the same stage of their careers. He's a well-made individual who did well to beat more experienced hurdlers in the Coral Golden Final at Cheltenham last season, a race, incidentally, Forgive N'Forget also won. Any potential chaser who can win a long-distance hurdle of that calibre has to be a good prospect. I feel it's also very much in Danny Connors' favour that he acts so well on fast ground, the majority of staying chasers don't; so he should, all being well, be able to gain valuable experience early on, if Jonjo decides he needs it.**

DESERT ORCHID

trained by
David Elsworth

**12 gr.g. Grey Mirage
Flower Child
(Brother)**

selected by
Jenny Pitman

Jenny Pitman's exploits as a National Hunt trainer have made her a household name. Formerly married to top National Hunt jockey Richard Pitman, Jenny began training at Weathercock House, Upper Lambourn in 1975. Her most successful season was in 1989/90 when she sent out ninety-three winners. She has trained a Grand National winner (Corbiere 1983) and two winners of the Gold Cup at Cheltenham (Burrough Hill Lad 1984, and Garrison Savannah 1991).   Jenny: **Well, I expect there will be a few raised eyebrows at my choice—Desert Orchid. If I'm honest I've chosen him mainly because I absolutely love him; how could any racing fan not! Come December and the King George at Kempton he's going to be exceptionally hard to beat. I've got some cracking staying chasers in my team but those and anyone else's will have to be spot on to take that King George from him. Even though he beat Toby Tobias of mine into second place last season I still went over to Dessie and gave him a pat; he's a horse in a million.**

GOLDEN CELTIC

trained by
Henrietta Knight

7 b.g. Rare One
Cooleen (Tarqogan)

selected by
Oliver Sherwood

Thirty-six-year-old Oliver Sherwood trains at Rhonehurst Stables, Upper Lambourn. Formerly assistant to Arthur Moore in Ireland and Fred Winter, he was champion amateur rider in 1979/80. Oliver, who began training in 1984, had his most successful season in 1989/90 when he trained fifty-eight winners.   Oliver: **Golden Celtic, trained by Henrietta Knight, is a horse that took my eye on several occasions last season. He won four of his seven races in novice chases and, really, was unlucky not to have won six—on two occasions he had races at Wolverhampton and Uttoxeter sewn up when coming to grief. Basically he's a fine jumper who seems to go particularly well on soft ground. He'll be a tough opponent in decent chases at up to three miles.**

JODAMI

trained by
Peter Beaumont

**6 b.g. Crash Course
Masterstown Lucy
(Bargello)**

selected by

Kim Bailey, Charlie Brooks & Gordon Richards

Kim Bailey has been training for more than thirteen years, having gained valuable experience as assistant to Tim Forster and the late Fred Rimell. Kim's best total of winners trained is thirty-four, gained in 1989/90, the same season in which his Mr Frisk won the Grand National. Kim: **Jodami is the sort of horse any trainer would love to have; he did tremendously well last year. Considering his stamina it's surprising that he was able to win over two miles earlier in the season. I think his last performance in a big novice handicap over two and three quarter miles at Ayr impressed everyone who was there. I ran a horse in the race but neither he nor any of the others got a look in.**

Charlie Brooks took over the licence at Uplands, Upper Lambourn, in 1988 after ill health forced the premature retirement of his then 'guvnor' Fred Winter. Charlie's now had three seasons in charge, the most successful of those his second, 1989/90, with 56 winners. Charlie: **Jodami will make a super chaser. He's got great strength and scope but, unlike a lot of big, strong horses, has shown both speed and stamina over hurdles. He's a great prospect.**

Gordon Richards was granted a trainer's licence in 1964. Since that time he's enjoyed tremendous success with numerous winners and a string of big-race successes to his credit, including two Grand Nationals (Lucius 1978, and Hallo Dandy 1984). Last season Gordon trained one hundred and eighteen winners, his best yet. Gordon: **Now let me tell you if I could go and buy him tomorrow I would; he should be a lovely chaser. The first time I took notice of him was at Ayr in March when he gave twelve pounds to one I train called Another Dyer. He's not a bad animal yet Jodami beat him easily; this is a good 'oss all right.**

KING'S CURATE

trained by
Stan Mellor

**7 b.g. King's Ride
Parnessa
(The Parson)**

selected by
Martin Pipe

During the last few seasons Martin Pipe's achievements as a National Hunt trainer have been little short of amazing. Close attention to specific detail, first-class organisation plus sheer hard work and dedication have reaped spectacular rewards and ensured that Pipe has set new standards within the sport. 1975/6 was the last season that Martin's final total was lower than its predecessor. His best score was attained last season with 230 successes. Martin: **It wasn't difficult nominating King's Curate. Firstly, he's a high-class horse, and secondly, he was a thorn in our side in the premier event for staying hurdlers. I thought Run For Free, whom I train, had a wonderful chance in the BonusPrint Stayers' Hurdle at Cheltenham but this horse just pipped us, in as good a race as we had at the Festival. King's Curate seems to have almost unlimited reserves of stamina—in the end he just wore Run For Free down, and he beat the rest by upwards of ten lengths. He's a fine, big horse, too, and should definitely make a chaser.**

SUPER SENSE

trained by
Josh Gifford

**6 b.g. Pragmatic
Killonan Lass
(The Parson)**

selected by
David Elsworth

Having spent the first fifteen years of his adult life as a National Hunt jockey David Elsworth, now fifty-one, turned his hand to training. Granted a licence in 1978, he's enjoyed spectacular success since then with numerous big-race wins both on the Flat and over the sticks, of which Desert Orchid's magnificent achievements stand out. Dessie provided David with his first Cheltenham Gold Cup success in 1989, Rhyme 'N' Reason having won him his first Grand National a year earlier. David's highest total of National Hunt wins is fifty-four attained in 1988/9. David: **Now this horse could be something out of the ordinary. He's typical of a lot of horses that Josh gets. For one that looks and was bred to be a staying chaser he ran a fantastic race in the Sun Alliance Novices' Hurdle at Cheltenham; didn't he come up that hill! He didn't have a hard season and looks open to plenty of improvement. If he turns out as expected don't you forget who told you so! Whether he stays over hurdles or goes over fences I don't think matters. The point is that the best is yet to come.**

IN PERSPECTIVE

The daily reports of Timeform's men on the course form the basis of Timeform Perspective. Their penetrating observations, supplemented by those of Timeform's handicappers and comment writers, make Timeform Perspective thoroughly informative. Here are the key performances from last season highlighted by the Timeform Form-Book.

Kempton December 26   Good to Soft
King George VI Rank Chase (5yo +)   3m

DESERT ORCHID 11-11-10 RDunwoody	9/4f		1
TOBY TOBIAS 8-11-10 MPitman	4/1	12	2
THE FELLOW (FR) 5-11-10 AKondrat	10/1	5	3
Celtic Shot 8-11-10 GMcCourt	11/4	7	4
Sabin du Loir (Fr) 11-11-10 MPerrett	7/1		f
Espy 7-11-10 BdeHaan	33/1		pu
Nick The Brief 8-11-10 RSupple	10/1		pu
Panto Prince 9-11-10 BPowell	33/1		pu
Prize Asset 10-11-10 SEarle	100/1		pu

Mr R. Burridge (D. R. C. Elsworth) 9ran 6m12.04

DESERT ORCHID puts up another tip-top performance in winning this event for the fourth time, but he'll find things harder on the next occasion when he'll be up against the likes of Blazing Walker and Remittance Man . . . . .

King George VI Rank Chase—Desert Orchid wins it for the fourth time

Trafalgar House Supreme Novices' Hurdle (4yo +)   2m (Old)

DESTRIERO 5-11-8 PMcWilliams	6/1		1
GRANVILLE AGAIN 5-11-8 PScudamore	2/1f	4	2
GRAN ALBA (USA) 5-11-8 GMcCourt	25/1	¾	3
Nordic Surprise 4-11-0 MrEJKearnsJun	6/1	5	4
General Idea 6-11-8 BSheridan	5/1	2	5
Book of Gold 6-11-8 DJMurphy	25/1	1	6
Trimlough 6-11-8 JJQuinn	100/1	1½	7
Bounden Duty (USA) 5-11-8 MPerrett	20/1	10	8
Shannon Glen 5-11-8 MPitman	25/1	1½	9
Johnny Will 6-11-8 JOsborne	100/1	1	10
Sabaki River 7-11-8 BPowell	33/1	sh	11
Hurricane Hugo 5-11-8 EMurphy	100/1	1	12
Charlton Yeoman 6-11-8 EMcKinley	66/1	¾	13
Done Instantly 6-11-8 MrTMullins	66/1	4	14
Viceroy Jester 6-11-8 NMann	100/1	2	15
Tasman Oak (NZ) 5-11-8 RHyett	100/1		16
Luthior (Fr) 5-11-8 (b) WMorris	500/1		17
New Duds (USA) 7-11-8 JLower	12/1		18
Chester Terrace 7-11-8 ACarroll	300/1		19
Storm Island 6-11-8 NWilliamson	200/1		20
Gaasid 6-11-8 LHarvey	14/1		su

Mrs Elizabeth Furlong (A. Geraghty) 21ran 3m58.04

In the last eight years, we rate only Vagador's performance in winning this race three years ago better than that of DESTRIERO. Furthermore, considering this was only his second competitive outing over hurdles, Destriero certainly has the potential to

Destriero leads into the straight

develop into a leading hurdler; apart from an error at the last, his hurdling was excellent for one with such limited experience. GRANVILLE AGAIN had anything but a good run, but we're fairly sure he wouldn't have beaten the winner anyway; he's a high-class hurdler in the making . . . . .

Cheltenham March 12   Good
Waterford Castle Arkle Challenge Trophy Chase (5yo+)   2m (Old)

REMITTANCE MAN 7-11-8 RDunwoody	85/40f		1
UNCLE ERNIE 6-11-8 MDwyer	5/2	6	2
REDUNDANT PAL 8-11-8 CO'Dwyer	16/1	6	3
Devil's Valley 8-11-8 (b) MPitman	25/1	5	4
Orbis (USA) 5-11-0 CFSwan	11/1	hd	5
My Young Man 6-11-8 JOsborne	11/1	5	6
Monumental Lad 8-11-8 RBellamy	40/1	12	7
General James 8-11-8 GBradley	50/1	20	8
Firions Law 6-11-8 KO'Brien	20/1	15	9
Geostar 7-11-8 GaryLyons	200/1		f
Last 'o' The Bunch 7-11-8 NDoughty	11/2		f
Buck Willow 7-11-8 DJMurphy	20/1		bd
Barkisland 7-11-8 NWilliamson	40/1		pu
Duke de Vendome 8-11-8 SSmithEccles	40/1		pu

Mr J. E. H. Collins (N. J. Henderson) 14ran 3m55.05

A thoroughly representative field, the winners of thirty-three novice chases, three of them unbeaten in five starts. REMITTANCE MAN, in particular, looks a top-notch chaser in the making; the chances are he'll be up to winning more good-class races over two miles, but he'll be more effective still returned to two and a half, or even three miles; anyway, he seems sure to play a major role in the best company, and we'd go so far as to say he'll prove a horse to rank alongside some of the greats. UNCLE ERNIE's performance fully

Remittance Man has the measure of Uncle Ernie

43

confirmed the favourable impression he's made this season; he's less of a stayer than the winner, but, with that horse likely to be campaigned over further, Uncle Ernie should have a bright future in good-class two-mile chases . . . . .

Cheltenham March 12 Good
Smurfit Champion Hurdle Challenge Trophy (4yo +) 2m (Old)

MORLEY STREET 7-12-0 JFrost	4/1f		1
NOMADIC WAY (USA) 6-12-0 (b) RDunwooody	9/1	1½	2
RULING (USA) 5-12-0 PNiven	50/1	hd	3
Mole Board 9-12-0 CLlewellyn	66/1	5	4
Voyage Sans Retour (Fr) 6-12-0 (b) JLower	33/1	1½	5
Bradbury Star 6-12-0 EMurphy	66/1	nk	6
Wonder Man (Fr) 6-12-0 BdeHaan	50/1	6	7
Beech Road 9-12-0 RichardGuest	8/1	2½	8
Royal Derbi 6-12-0 TCarmody	66/1	12	9
Deep Sensation 6-12-0 DJMurphy	50/1	¾	10
Jinxy Jack 7-12-0 NDoughty	16/1	½	11
Athy Spirit 6-12-0 TTaaffe	10/1	2½	12
Rare Holiday 5-12-0 BSheridan	50/1	¾	13
Vayrua (Fr) 6-12-0 MPerrett	33/1	1	14
Philosophos 5-12-0 NColeman	250/1		15
Riverhead (USA) 7-12-0 PHolley	50/1		16
Danny Harrold 7-12-0 (b) MPitman	16/1		17
Vestris Abu 5-12-0 CFSwan	33/1		18
Major Inquiry (USA) 5-12-0 GBradley	66/1		19
Sondrio 10-12-0 PScudamore	10/1		20
The Illiad 10-12-0 PMcWilliams	11/2		21
Black Humour 7-12-0 JOsborne	20/1		f
Fidway 6-12-0 (b) SSmithEccles	15/2		ur
Sybillin 5-12-0 MDwyer	20/1		pu

Michael Jackson Bloodstock Ltd (G. B. Balding) 24ran 3m54.31

It wasn't a vintage line-up by any means, as no less than nine of the runners had failed to win a race this season and only MORLEY STREET had recorded a level of performance normally required to win a Champion Hurdle; his manner of victory was workmanlike rather than impressive, but there's reason for believing he's capable of better than the bare result would imply and he's undoubtedly the best hurdler around. NOMADIC WAY (USA) ran another gallant race to finish second for the second year running, performing every bit as well as in 1990. The entire RULING (USA) did astonishingly well for a lightly-raced novice, particularly considering his hurdling technique is, as yet, nowhere near so accomplished as that of the likes of Morley Street or Nomadic Way; his future looks a very bright one indeed . . . . .

Champion Hurdler Morley Street

Cheltenham March 12   Good
BonusPrint Stayers' Hurdle (4yo +)   3m1f

KING'S CURATE 7-11-10 MPerrett........................ 5/2f   1
RUN FOR FREE 7-11-10 PScudamore................ 11/4   nk 2
PRAGADA 8-11-10 DJMurphy............................ 12/1   10 3
Judges Fancy 7-11-10 RSupple 40/1 1½ 4
Galmoy 12-11-10 TCarmody................................ 16/1   25 5
Mutare 6-11-10 RDunwoody................................9/2 2½ 6
Do Be Brief 6-11-10 (b) MPitman 10/1   6 7

King's Curate (far side) and Run For Free

45

Old Dundalk 7-11-10 (v) GBradley........................25/1   6   8
Holding Scent 5-11-10 CFSwan..........................14/1   8   9
Cash Is King 7-11-10 (b) DGallagher....................25/1 1½ 10
Buckskin's Best 9-11-10 SEarle ....150/1 ¾ 11
Calapaez 7-11-10 BPowell..................................25/1   6 12
Olnistar (Fr) 5-11-5 GMcCourt ....50/1   f
Calabrese 6-11-10 JWhite....................................25/1   pu
Grand Habit 7-11-10 CO'Dwyer ....150/1   pu

Mr C. J. Ells (S. Mellor) 15ran 6m33.50

A cracking spectacle, with the heavily-backed KING'S CURATE getting up on the run-in after looking a most unlikely winner for the vast majority of the journey; a big, good-topped gelding, he has the physical attributes one looks for in a high-class chaser and he should do well as a staying novice in 1991/2 . . . . .

Cheltenham March 13   Good
Sun Alliance Novices' Hurdle (4yo +)   2½m (Old)

CRYSTAL SPIRIT 4-10-12 JFrost........................2/1f   1
MINORETTES GIRL 6-11-2 AMullins 4/1   4   2
SUPER SENSE 6-11-7 DJMurphy 40/1   2   3
South Harvest 8-11-7 RJBeggan 16/1   5   4
Egypt Mill Prince 5-11-7 MPitman......................20/1   8   5
Upton Park 6-11-7 BPowell.................................14/1   hd   6
Tyrone Bridge 5-11-7 (b) PScudamore ....10/1   hd   7
Rocktor (NZ) 6-11-7 NHawke.............................66/1   2   8
Saddler's Choice 6-11-7 NWilliamson 25/1 2½   9
One More Knight 8-11-7 JDuggan 25/1   3 10
Black Sapphire 4-10-12 PNiven 100/1 2½ 11
Moze Tidy 6-11-7 MDwyer 50/1 1½ 12
Your Well 5-11-7 BMClifford...............................40/1   sh 13
Estwing (NZ) 8-11-7 JacquiOliver 100/1   14
Secret Four 5-11-7 LHarvey................................33/1   15
Juranstan 6-11-7 SJO'Neill 500/1   16
Yeoman Metro 7-11-7 EMcKinley......................66/1   17
Strong Beau 6-11-7 RDunwoody.........................33/1   18
Shadow Run 6-11-7 GMcCourt...........................200/1   19
Master Dancer 4-10-12 AJQuinn 50/1   20
Cache Fleur (Fr) 5-11-7 JLower 33/1   21
Captain Dibble 6-11-7 CLlewellyn........................16/1   22
Blazing Touch (USA) 5-11-7 (b) BdeHaan 100/1   23
Mister Gebo 6-11-7 DTegg.................................66/1   24
Ballyanto 6-11-7 NDawe 250/1   25
Burgoyne 5-11-7 LWyer.......................................25/1   pu
Change The Act 6-11-7 JOsborne ....14/1   pu

Crystal Spirit leads Minorettes Girl

Highgate Mild 6-11-7 STurner .... 500/1   pu
Soupcon 5-11-2 DaleMcKeown .... 200/1   pu

Mr Paul Mellon (I. A. Balding) 29ran 5m04.58

CRYSTAL SPIRIT and MINORETTES GIRL both came into this race with form of the standard required to win an average Sun Alliance Novices' Hurdle and dominated the betting; in winning, Crystal Spirit (the third four-year-old to succeed following Sabin du Loir in 1983 and Fealty in 1984) once again confirmed he's a very useful staying hurdler, and should all go well in the meantime he'll become a force to be reckoned with in the top long-distance events in 1991/2 including, of course, the three-mile championship here . . . . .

Cheltenham March 14   Good
Daily Express Triumph Hurdle (4yo)   2m (New)

OH SO RISKY 4-11-0 PHolley 14/1   1
CHIRKPAR 4-11-0 LPCusack 5/1   12 2
BOARDING SCHOOL 4-11-0 TCarmody 33/1 2½ 3
Runway Romance (Fr) 4-11-0 GMcCourt 66/1   4 4
Olympian 4-11-0 (b) WMcFarland 16/1   1 5
Legal Beagle 4-11-0 MPerrett 16/1 2½ 6
Persuasive 4-10-9 MDwyer .... 66/1   ¾ 7

Bottles (USA) 4-11-0 RichardGuest 33/1 5 8
Hopscotch 4-10-9 PScudamore 7/2f 3 9
Cornwall Prince 4-11-0 DJMurphy 20/1 5 10
Cheering News 4-11-0 BSheridan 14/1 2½ 11
Pashto 4-11-0 RDunwoody .... 9/1 nk 12
Bold Street Blues 4-11-0 CSmith .... 250/1 nk 13
Woodside Heath 4-11-0 ACharlton .... 100/1 nk 14
French Ivy (USA) 4-11-0 CLlewellyn 150/1 7 15
Access Sun 4-11-0 JRKavanagh .... 66/1 nk 16
Galevilla Express 4-10-9 CNBowens 50/1 2½ 17
Champagne Gold 4-11-0 JShortt 18/1 3 18
Belafonte 4-11-0 (b) EMByrne .... 66/1 ½ 19
Kibreet 4-11-0 GBradley 33/1   20
Keppols Prince 4-11-0 APowell 40/1   21
Stanway 4-11-0 MMLynch 200/1   22
Tomahawk 4-11-0 NMann 12/1   23
Nordic Surprise 4-11-0 MrEJKearnsJun 11/1   24
Triumphal Song 4-11-0 BPowell 66/1   25
Gilded Past 4-11-0 WWorthington .... 500/1   f
Srivijaya 4-11-0 JOsborne .... 66/1   pu

The Oh So Risky Syndicate (D. R. C. Elsworth) 27ran 4m01.45
Not a vintage 'Triumph', but Oh So Risky could hardly have been
more impressive and he looks a good prospect . . . . .

Oh So Risky is out on his own

Tote Cheltenham Gold Cup Chase (5yo +)   3¼m (New)

GARRISON SAVANNAH 8-12-0 (b)
MPitman 16/1   1
THE FELLOW (FR) 6-12-0 AKondrat .... 28/1   sh 2
DESERT ORCHID 12-12-0 RDunwoody 4/1   15 3
Cool Ground 9-12-0 LHarvey 7/1 2½ 4
Kildimo 11-12-0 RStronge .... 66/1   hd 5
Nick The Brief 9-12-0 RSupple 12/1 2½ 6
Celtic Shot 9-12-0 PScudamore 5/2f   2 7
Yahoo 10-12-0 (b) NWilliamson 100/1   8
Norton's Coin 10-12-0 GMcCourt .... 16/1   f
Arctic Call 8-12-0 (b) JOsborne .... 10/1   pu
Party Politics 7-12-0 AAdams .... 33/1   pu
Carrick Hill Lad 8-12-0 MDwyer .... 11/1   pu
Martin d'Or (Fr) 7-12-0 J-NJoly .... 250/1   pu
Twin Oaks 11-12-0 NDoughty .... 11/1   pu

Autofour Engineering (Mrs J. Pitman) 14ran 6m49.81

A Gold Cup which provided a race full of excitement, even though the principals weren't those widely expected, and for the future it was good to see two of the younger brigade dominate the finish. GARRISON SAVANNAH showed considerably improved form to emerge a narrow winner; he's sure to be difficult to beat in top company, and probably has more improvement in him. So, too, does THE FELLOW (FR), who ran a tremendous race as a six-year-old, and deserves even more credit considering he made a bad mistake at the fifteenth. DESERT ORCHID gave his all, but just doesn't seem the same horse going left-handed . . . . .

Garrison Savannah (blinkers) and The Fellow battle it out

2299

£81,790	**Smurfit Champion Hurdle** 2m (8) (Old) Challenge Trophy (Grade 1) (4yo+)		
2139	MORLEY STREET 7-12-0 JFrost	4/1f	1
2132	NOMADIC WAY (USA) 6-12-0 (b) RDunwoody	9/1	1½ 2
1778	RULING (USA) 5-12-0 PNiven	50/1	hd 3
1956	Mole Board 9-12-0 CLlewellyn	66/1	5 4
1894	Voyage Sans Retour (Fr) 6-12-0 (b) JLower	33/1	1½ 5
1987	Bradbury Star 6-12-0 EMurphy	66/1	nk 6
1894	Wonder Man (Fr) 6-12-0 BdeHaan	50/1	6 7
1956	Beech Road 9-12-0 RichardGuest	8/1	2½ 8
2152	Royal Derbi 6-12-0 TCarmody	66/1	12 9
1956	Deep Sensation 6-12-0 DJMurphy	50/1	¾ 10
2017	Jinxy Jack 7-12-0 NDoughty	16/1	½ 11
1901	Athy Spirit 6-12-0 TTaaffe	10/12½ 12	
1952	Rare Holiday 5-12-0 BSheridan	50/1	¾ 13
1253	Vayrua (Fr) 6-12-0 MPerrett	33/1	1 14
1694	Philosophos 5-12-0 NColeman	250/1	15
2132	Riverhead (USA) 7-12-0 PHolley	50/1	16
2139	Danny Harrold 7-12-0 (b) MPitman	16/1	17
	Vestris Abu (USA) 6-12-0 CFSwan	33/1	18
2008	Major Inquiry (USA) 5-12-0 GBradley	66/1	19
2132	Sondrio 10-12-0 PScudamore	10/1	20
1674	The Illiad 10-12-0 PMcWilliams	11/2	21
2025	Black Humour 7-12-0 JOsborne	20/1	f
1894	Fidway 6-12-0 (b) SSmithEccles	15/2	ur
2152	Sybillin 5-12-0 MDwyer	20/1	pu

Michael Jackson Bloodstock Ltd (G. B. Balding) 24ran 3m54.31

The joint-biggest field for a Champion Hurdle and a very open-looking contest, with none of the protagonists having staked a clear-cut claim to the title in their preparatory races. It wasn't a vintage line-up by any means, as no less than nine of the runners had failed to win a race this season and only MORLEY STREET had recorded a level of performance normally required to win a Champion Hurdle; to complicate matters slightly further, this was his first outing over two miles since he finished fifth behind Kribensis a year ago. In the event, Morley Street's manner of victory was workmanlike rather than impressive, but there's reason for believing he's capable of better than the bare result would imply; he looked well in the paddock, though a shade warm, and showed a fluent action to post; held up two-thirds of the way down the field in a race run at a good gallop, he began to close on the leaders along the far side, jumping hurdles three, four and five particularly fluently, and was full of running at the top of the hill in sixth or seventh position; a mistake at the third from home cost him a length or so, but he ranged alongside the leaders at the penultimate flight and quickened clear turning for home; he went left and ran down the final hurdle, then drifted back to his right when shaken up and, not for the first time, began to idle; he tied up noticeably halfway up the run-in and had absolutely nothing left in reserve at the finish; Morley Street is blessed with a fine turn of foot, and had Jimmy Frost held him up longer instead of kicking on turning for home he'd have been a more impressive winner, though in no way are we implying any criticism of the jockey; he's undoubtedly the best hurdler around, and will take all the beating at Liverpool, where he attempts to follow up last season's impressive victory in the Sandeman Aintree Hurdle. Toby Balding deserves great credit for bringing Morley Street back from a broken blood vessel and an abortive chasing career. The entire, NOMADIC WAY (USA), ran another gallant race to finish second for the second year running, and performed every bit as well as when

Save a third on the full price of Timeform Ratings
PERSPECTIVE & RATINGS

Timeform Perspective and another of the famous Timeform services the Timeform Race Ratings can now be purchased together at a special price, saving **over a third on the full-season price of the Race Ratings Service** if you order Timeform Perspective at the same time. The Timeform Race Ratings Booklets provide an invaluable handicap analysis of each race—more than half of all winners in the 1990/1 season were in Timeform's two top-rated—and include a reference number so that you can easily check the recent performances of all the runners in Timeform Perspective. Here are just a couple of examples:-

Timeform Perspective

2042

£10,210	Galloway Braes Novices' Chase (Grade 2) (5yo +)	2½m (17)	
1354	REMITTANCE MAN 7-11-7 RDunwoody	10/3	1
1757	MONUMENTAL LAD 8-11-3 RBellamy.............	20/1	30 2
1891	REPEAT THE DOSE 6-11-3 BPowell	11/2	12 3
1801	Geostar 7-11-3 GaryLyons	33/1	12 4
1711	File Concord 7-11-3 MPitman	15/8f	f
1720	Trefelyn Cove 7-10-12 PScudamore	85/40	f
1647	Bignor Hill 6-11-3 EMcKinley	33/1	bd
1817	Amrullah 11-11-3 (v) GMoore......................	100/1	pu

Mr J. E. H. Collins (N. J. Henderson) 8ran 5m14.02

Despite two of the field departing at the first, this developed into a really good test and produced a most impressive performance from the winner. REMITTANCE MAN looked a really exciting prospect in routing a good field and putting up his best effort yet; he raced in touch travelling well, jumped into the lead at the twelfth, gained lengths at each of the five remaining fences, and went clear on the bridle in the straight; it is seldom you see a novice jump with a much confidence and zest, and it will take a good performance to better him at two and a half miles; his target is the Arkle, and he had only one race in the past two seasons over two miles, but he shows plenty of pace in his races, his jumping will stand him in good stead, and he must go to Cheltenham with a first-rate chance. MONUMENTAL LAD, who was held up, was outpaced from the ninth, but jumped well down the back straight the final time and gradually recovered ground, though he had no chance with the winner and was struggling about three lengths behind File Concord

'His target is the Arkle and he must go to Cheltenham with a first-rate chance' — Clear top-rated REMITTANCE MAN WON 85–40

Timeform Perspective

889

£3,556	St Mary's Trial Hurdle (4, 5 and 6yo)	2m (8)	
	DEEP SENSATION 5-11-3 RRowe....................	10/11f	1
	ATLAAL 5-11-0 MAhern³	14/1	¾ 2
618	SPRING HAY 4-11-3 RDunwoody...................	7/4	15 3
	Villa Recos 5-10-12 MBowlby.....................	14/1	½ 4
	Nickle Joe 4-10-8 DGallagher....................500/1		25 5
615	Bolshoi Boy 6-10-12 RHyett........................50/1		5 6
686	Jimstro 5-10-8 ACarroll ....500/1 dist 7		
	Wonder Man (Fr) 5-11-3 MPitman	14/1	f
725	Susan's Reef 5-10-8 DTegg.........................500/1		pu

Mr R. F. Eliot (J. T. Gifford) 9ran 3m45.64

As the title suggests, this wasn't as competitive a race as it might have looked on paper, with at least four of the field using it as preparation for bigger targets ahead, and it duly turned out to be an interesting contest with an eye to the future ... ATLAAL stayed on strongly, the William Hill Handicap Hurdle in two weeks' time is his probable next engagement, but we're more interested in WONDER MAN (FR) for that race; he was within a length of Atlaal, still appearing to have plenty of running left in him, when he clipped the top of the second last and fell; he looked a bit backward, and there's a good chance he's much better than the mark he'll race off at Sandown, so, provided the ground isn't riding firm, which might be against him judged on his previous record, he has prospects of making valuable amends for this mishap. Another one for the notebook, particularly in handicaps, is his stable-

'He has prospects of making valuable amends for this mishap in the William Hill Handicap in two weeks time' — Clear top-rated WONDER MAN WON 11–4

Timeform Race Ratings

2.50 2m Chase

ARKLE CHALLENGE TROPHY
TRW 157 152 169 159 154
(Average 158)

2184	Barkisland	116p
1631	Buck Willow	138p
2064	Devil's Valley	114p
1394	Duke de Vendome	133
1951	Firions Law	148
1705	General James	132
2042	Geostar	127
2147	Last 'o' The Bunch	143p
2042	Monumental Lad	131
2030	My Young Man	141p
2168	Redundant Pal	143?
2042	Remittance Man	155p
2151	Uncle Ernie	149p
2169	Orbis	149p

Timeform Race Ratings

2.00 2m Hcp Hurdle

WILLIAM HILL HANDICAP

	Yaheeb	11-12	–
770	Stratford Ponds	11-10	147
999	Atlaal	11-9	152
874	Peanuts Pet	11-3	155
786	Liadett	11-3	155
	Persian Style	10-13	151
889	Wonder Man	10-12	151
794	Without A D'bt	10-12	162
786	Highland B'nty	10-10	152
689	Coe	10-7	153
1003	Elegant Stranger	10-7	150
973	Arastou	10-0	148§
		10-0	138

SUBSCRIPTION RATES

TIMEFORM PERSPECTIVE
1991/92 Chase £179
(for limited period only—full price £209)
or £59 downpayment and four instalments of £30 each (due Nov 1, Dec 1, Jan 1, Feb 1)

Surcharges for delivery abroad (£ sterling) by letter rate, Irish Republic and European countries £30; other overseas rates on application.

PERSPECTIVE & RATINGS COMBINED
1991/92 Chase £419
(saves over a third on full price of Timeform Race Ratings)
or £179 downpayment and four instalments of £60 each (due Nov 1, Dec 1, Jan 1, Feb 1)

Perspective & Ratings postal subscription is only available to UK customers

The Combined Subscription is also available to customers with a fax or telex facility (Perspective by post; Race Ratings service—declared runners—transmitted day before racing).

Order TODAY by credit card on (0422) 330540 (24-hr line)
or by post from
1 Timeform House   Halifax
West Yorkshire   HX1 1XE

Fax (0422) 358645   Telex (0422) 51353

The Timeform Perspective analysis covers all jump racing (turf and all-weather) between Saturday October 5 1991 and Saturday April 4 1992 (Grand National Day); the binder (including all results from August) will be posted to subscribers on Wednesday October 9 and parts will follow weekly thereafter to provide a complete race-by-race, meeting-by-meeting record of the results of all races over the sticks in Britain in the 1991/92 season (Timeform Perspective analysis will continue for selected meetings and big races after Grand National day). The Timeform Race Ratings Service, which is published in booklet form and posted usually four times a week, provides Timeform Race Ratings (already adjusted for weights carried) race-by-race for each meeting at the 5-day stage and covers all meetings between Monday November 4 1991 and Saturday May 30 1992. Timeform Perspective is available only by subscribing to the end of the season, but can be purchased from any point during the season (with the Race Ratings Service or on its own)

The perceptive comments of Timeform Perspective and the pinpoint accuracy of Timeform Ratings!

Welsh Champion Hurdle (4yo +)   2m

WONDER MAN (FR) 6-11-10 MPitman 4/1   1
VOYAGE SANS RETOUR (FR) 6-11-10 (b)
   CLlewellyn 2/1f   4   2
BOKARO (FR) 5-12-1 GBradley 7/1   10   3
Philosophos 5-12-1 NColeman 25/1   4   4
Welsh Bard 7-12-1 JWhite 12/1   12   5
Riverhead (USA) 7-11-6 PHolley 10/1   5   6
Beech Road 9-12-1 RichardGuest 7/2   20   7
Olveston (NZ) 7-11-6 HDavies 9/1   8

Mrs Shirley Robins (Mrs J. Pitman) 8ran 3m50.83

The speedy WONDER MAN has developed into a very smart
hurdler and looks an ideal candidate for the Top Rank Christmas
Hurdle at Kempton in 1991/2. In the longer term, he's a cracking
chaser in the making . . . . .

Wonder Man has the race sewn up

Glenlivet Anniversary Hurdle (4yo)   2m

MONTPELIER LAD 4-11-0 NDoughty 9/1   1
RUNWAY ROMANCE (FR) 4-11-0 GMcCourt 11/1 2½ 2
NATIVE MISSION 4-11-0 MDwyer 8/1   5   3
Silken Fan (USA) 4-11-0 MRichards 33/1 1½ 4
Hopscotch 4-10-13 PScudamore 6/1 1½ 5
Chirkpar 4-11-0 LPCusack 9/4f   3   6

Pashto 4-11-0 RDunwoody....................................11/1 7 7
Galway Star 4-11-0 AMullins 50/1 8
Beau Rou 4-11-0 (v) BPowell.......................... 150/1 f
Wake Up 4-11-0 LWyer .... 100/1 ur
Albertito (Fr) 4-11-0 GaryLyons......................... 100/1 bd
Reve de Valse (USA) 4-11-0 CGrant......................4/1 bd
Cornwall Prince 4-11-0 (b) DJMurphy .... 14/1 pu
Marlingford 4-11-0 DMorris ....20/1 pu

Mr David T. Little (G. Richards) 14ran 4m09.90

Gordon Richards told us in the *Timeform Interview* that he
regarded MONTPELIER LAD as the best hurdling prospect he'd
had since Sea Pigeon; Montpelier Lad is unlikely to stay much
further than two miles, but has more scope than most of this field
and there's no reason why he shouldn't make up into a good
hurdler. RUNWAY ROMANCE (FR) looked well and turned in
another good effort; he might be difficult to place in 1991/2, though
judged on this he's still improving . . . . .

Montpelier Lad takes command in the Glenlivet Anniversary Hurdle

Glenlivet Melling Chase (5yo +)   2½m

BLAZING WALKER 7-11-10 CGrant 5/1		1
KATABATIC 8-11-10 LHarvey 10/3	10	2
WATERLOO BOY 8-11-10 RDunwoody 7/2	2½	3
Sabin du Loir (Fr) 12-11-10 PScudamore 4/1	12	4
Barnbrook Again 10-11-10 HDavies 3/1f	30	5
Aston Express 8-11-10 (b) MDwyer 66/1		pu
Cuddy Dale 8-11-10 DJMurphy 66/1		pu

Mr P. Piller (W. A. Stephenson) 7ran 5m02.66

A tremendous race won in a most emphatic style by BLAZING
WALKER, who gave a performance which stamps him without
question as one of the leading chasers in this country; his
participation in the top-class events in 1991/2 is eagerly anticipated,
as this form entitles him to trouble any horse in the country—even
Desert Orchid at his best—in races such as the King George VI
Rank Chase at Kempton on Boxing Day. KATABATIC should
continue to hold his own in top company over two and two and a
half miles in 1991/2 . . . . .

Blazing Walker shows himself a top-class chaser

Sandeman Aintree Hurdle (4yo +)   2½m

MORLEY STREET 7-11-7 JFrost......................... 11/8f   1
NOMADIC WAY (USA) 6-11-7 (b)
  RDunwoody...7/2   6 2
RUN FOR FREE 7-11-7 PScudamore 5/1   5 3
Bradbury Star 6-11-7 DJMurphy......................... 18/1   sh 4
Mole Board 9-11-7 JOsborne 16/1   7 5
The Illiad 10-11-7 PMcWilliams........................... 10/1   ¾ 6
Jinxy Jack 7-11-7 GMcCourt............................... 25/1   ½ 7
Cloughtaney 10-11-7 AMullins.............................50/1   5 8
Fidway 6-11-7 (b) SSmithEccles 11/1   9

Michael Jackson Bloodstock Ltd (G. B. Balding) 9ran 4m54.48

Champion Hurdler MORLEY STREET well and truly spreadeagled his eight rivals, winning far more impressively than at Cheltenham—he's yet to put up a performance to match the likes of Night Nurse, Monksfield or Sea Pigeon, but then again he's yet to be tested to the full and may have further improvement in him; he'll remain very difficult to beat. NOMADIC WAY (USA) probably ran as well as at Cheltenham, though beaten further by the winner; he's reportedly to be campaigned over longer distances in 1991/2 and could well develop into a top-class stayer . . . . .

Michael Jackson Bloodstock Ltd's "Morley Street"

Seagram Grand National Chase (Handicap) (7yo +)   4½m

SEAGRAM (NZ) 11-10-6 NHawke 12/1		1
GARRISON SAVANNAH 8-11-1 (b) MPitman........ 7/1	5	2
AUNTIE DOT 10-10-4 MDwyer............................ 50/1	8	3
OVER THE ROAD 10-10-0 RSupple.................... 50/1	25	4
Bonanza Boy 10-11-7 PScudamore 13/2f	sh	5
Durham Edition 13-10-13 CGrant....................... 25/1	1½	6
Golden Minstrel 12-10-2 TGrantham 50/1	4	7
Old Applejack 11-10-1 TReed............................. 66/1	6	8
Leagaune 9-10-0 MRichards 200/1	2	9
Foyle Fisherman 12-10-0 EMurphy.................... 40/1	4	10
Ballyhane 10-10-3 DJMurphy............................ 22/1	12	11
Harley 11-10-0 GerLyons.................................. 150/1	1½	12
Mick's Star 11-10-0 CFSwan............................ 100/1	30	13
Ten of Spades 11-11-1 JWhite........................... 15/1	5	14
Forest Ranger 9-10-0 DTegg............................ 100/1		15
Yahoo 10-11-1 NWilliamson 33/1		16
Golden Freeze 9-11-0 MBowlby........................ 40/1		17
Rinus 10-10-7 NDoughty 7/1		f
Joint Sovereignty 11-10-0 LO'Hara 100/1		f
Run And Skip 13-10-0 DByrne........................... 66/1		f
Southernair 11-10-1 (b) MrJ-FSimo 100/1		f

Seagram Grand National Chase—the leaders at Becher's on the second circuit

Docklands Express 9-10-3 ATory .... 20/1   f
Crammer 11-10-2 MrJPDurkan .... 28/1   ur
Blue Dart 11-10-2 HDavies............................... 80/1   ur
The Langholm Dyer 12-10-6 GMcCourt .... 100/1   ur
New Halen 10-10-0 SJO'Neill .... 50/1   ur
Fraze (Cze) 8-11-10 MrVChaloupka.................. 100/1   pu
Mister Christian (NZ) 10-10-0 (b) SEarle........... 100/1   pu
Hotplate 8-10-2 PNiven .... 80/1   pu
Abba Lad 9-10-0 (b) DGallagher...................... 250/1   pu
Bumbles Folly (NZ) 10-10-5 JFrost.................. 150/1   pu
General Chandos 10-10-3 MrJBradburne......... 150/1   pu
Envopak Token 10-10-0 MPerrett...................... 28/1   pu
Huntworth 11-10-8 MrAWalter........................... 50/1   pu
Oklaoma II (Fr) 11-10-7 RKleparski .... 66/1   pu
Mr Frisk 12-11-6 MrMArmytage .... 25/1   pu
Master Bob 11-10-5 (v) JOsborne .... 20/1   pu
Bigsun 10-10-4 RDunwoody............................... 9/1   pu
Solidasarock 9-10-4 GBradley .... 50/1   pu
Team Challenge 9-10-0 (b) BdeHaan .... 50/1   ref

Sir Eric Parker (D. H. Barons) 40ran 9m29.93

SEAGRAM (NZ) looked booked for second over the last, but stayed on really strongly to hit the front about a hundred yards out. GARRISON SAVANNAH is probably not so effective over very long distances as he is at up to, say, three and a half miles, and he tired dramatically with about two hundred yards to run. AUNTIE DOT jumped particularly well and stayed on in game fashion for third. OVER THE ROAD ran really well from 11 lb out of the handicap, particularly as he made several mistakes . . . . .

Liverpool April 6   Good to Soft
Mumm Prize Novices' Hurdle (4yo +)   2½m

SHANNON GLEN 5-11-1 MBowlby...................... 8/1   1
CRYSTAL SPIRIT 4-11-2 JFrost.......................... 4/5f   8   2
SO PROUD 6-11-1 MPerrett 14/1   1   3
Gulsha 5-10-10 PScudamore 8/1   8   4
Nadiad 5-11-1 GMcCourt 50/1   8   5
Among Friends 6-11-1 GBradley.......................33/1   2½   6
Granvillewaterford 6-11-1 JOsborne................... 7/1   15   7
For Heaven's Sake (Fr) 6-11-1 DTegg................. 50/1   8
Bell Glass (Fr) 5-11-1 RDunwoody..................... 10/1   9

Mrs Elizabeth Hitchins (Mrs J. Pitman) 9ran 5m01.22

Crystal Spirit failed to reproduce his Cheltenham running. Nevertheless, SHANNON GLEN ran out an impressive winner, clearly benefiting from the step up in distance; he is open to further

Mumm Prize Novices' Hurdle—Shannon Glen draws away from Crystal Spirit

improvement over hurdles, but this son of Furry Glen (also sire of the same connections' Toby Tobias) has the build to come into his own when sent chasing . . . . .

Ascot April 10   Good to Firm

Golden Eagle Novices' Chase (5yo +)   2½m

SOUTHERLY BUSTER 8-11-4 (b) JOsborne 9/2   1
GIVUS A BUCK 8-11-4 (b) PHolley...................... 10/1   4 2

Southerly Buster at Ascot

ACRE HILL 7-11-8 RDunwoody 11/2 15 3
Man On The Line 8-11-4 LHarvey 20/1 3½ 4
Sea Island 7-10-13 GMcCourt .... 9/2 sh 5
Laundryman 8-11-11 MPerrett .... 13/8f   f
Bitter Buck 8-10-13 (b) GBradley .... 10/1   ref

Mr M. D. S. Dorey (O. Sherwood) 7ran 4m52.20

SOUTHERLY BUSTER jumps fences boldly and well, has plenty of scope for improving on his already fairly useful form and will be an interesting prospect in handicap chases in 1991/2 . . . . .

Cheltenham April 17   Good to Firm
South Wales Showers Caradon Mira
Silver Trophy Chase (5yo +) 2½m

NORTON'S COIN 10-11-4 GMcCourt 9/4   1
WATERLOO BOY 8-11-7 RDunwoody .... 9/4 hd 2
PEGWELL BAY 10-11-7 JRailton 13/8f 6 3
Aston Express 8-11-0 (b) GBradley 20/1 25 4

Mr S. G. Griffiths (Owner) 4ran 5m26.49

A sprint finish between two high-class chasers who'll both continue to give a good account of themselves in 1991/2. NORTON'S COIN, who needs exaggerated waiting tactics, has a fine turn of speed, especially for one who stays three and a quarter miles. WATERLOO BOY, runner-up in the last two runnings of the Queen Mother Champion Chase at Cheltenham, will again be a leading contender for that race in 1992 . . . . .

From left to right—Norton's Coin, Waterloo Boy and Pegwell Bay

Whitbread Gold Cup (Handicap Chase) (5yo +)   3m5f18y

Order as they passed the post

CAHERVILLAHOW 7-11-2 CFSwan	4/1jf		1
DOCKLANDS EXPRESS 9-10-3 ATory	4/1jf	¾	2
WONT BE GONE LONG 9-10-0 RDunwoody	7/1	5	3
Seagram (NZ) 11-10-6 NHawke	9/2	½	4
Omerta 11-10-1 PScudamore	6/1	10	5
Durham Edition 13-10-0 CGrant	8/1	4	6
Vulgan Warrior 9-10-0 MBowlby	9/1	25	7
Bonanza Boy 10-11-7 SSmithEccles	25/1		pu
Ten of Spades 11-10-12 JWhite	20/1		pu
Tuns Hill 9-10-0 SEarle	50/1		pu

Mr R. H. Baines (K. C. Bailey) 10ran 7m16.90

As ever, the Whitbread provided a cracking spectacle and ultimately a controversial outcome, with the first past the post Cahervillahow being disqualified in favour of Docklands Express. CAHERVILLAHOW jumped into the lead at the last and ran on really strongly to win decisively; but he drifted persistently right up the run-in, carrying the second with him. DOCKLANDS EXPRESS is clearly still on the upgrade and should continue to give a very good account of himself in valuable staying handicaps in 1991/2 . . . . .

Cahervillahow (right) and Docklands Express are just ahead of Seagram at the last

THE TIMEFORM
TOP CHASERS AND HURDLERS

Here are listed the 'Top 100' in the Chasers & Hurdlers Annual

Chasers

178	Desert Orchid
173	Blazing Walker
171	Garrison Savannah
171	The Fellow
170	Celtic Shot
166	Toby Tobias
165	Katabatic
163	Waterloo Boy
162	Cahervillahow
162	Nick The Brief
161§	Norton's Coin
161	Bonanza Boy
161	Carrick Hill Lad
161	Carvill's Hill
158	Blitzkreig
158	Cool Ground
158	Young Snugfit
157	Pegwell Bay
157	Sabin du Loir
155§	Kildimo
155	Arctic Call
155	Seagram
154	Boutzdaroff
154	Twin Oaks
153p	Remittance Man
153	Mr Frisk
153	The Thinker
152§	Nos Na Gaoithe
152	Aquilifer
152	Kiichi
152	Star's Delight
151p	Young Benz
151	Larchmont
150p	Sparkling Flame
150d	Yahoo
150	Have A Barney
149p	Docklands Express
149§	Redundant Pal
149	Roc de Prince
148	Comandante
147	Gold Options
147	Man O'Magic
147	Uncle Ernie
147	Wingspan
146	Omerta
146	Ten of Spades
145?	Saffron Lord
145	Panto Prince
145	Us And Joe
144p	Party Politics
144	Rinus
143?	Beau Ranger
143?	Mystic Music
143	Auntie Dot
143	Chatam
143	Ida's Delight
142p	Master Rajh
142	Bigsun
142	Midnight Train
142	Sam da Vinci
141	Bluff Knoll
141	Field Conqueror
141	Garamycin
141	Last 'o' The Bunch
141	Von Csadek
141	Wont Be Gone Long
140p	Rolling Ball
140	Golden Freeze
140x	Boraceva
139d	Joint Sovereignty
139	Master Bob
138	Cuddy Dale
138	Durham Edition
138	Huntworth
137 +	Southern Minstrel
137?	Copperite
137	Esha Ness
137	Four Trix
137	Full Strength
137	Fu's Lady
137	Multum In Parvo
137	Tartan Tailor
137	Whats The Crack
136	Antinous
136	Devil's Valley
136	Foyle Fisherman
136	Golden Celtic
136	Hogmanay
136	Killone Abbey
136	One More Knight
136	Pat's Jester
135p	Good For A Laugh
135	Cushinstown
135	Greenheart
135	Orbis
135	Playschool
135	Rawhide
135	Rowlandsons Jewels
135	Solidasarock
135	Tartan Takeover

Hurdlers

174	Morley Street
168	Nomadic Way
167	Ruling
164	King's Curate
163	Bradbury Star
163	Run For Free
162	Mole Board
161	Grabel
161	Voyage Sans Retour
159	Trapper John
157 +	Wonder Man
157?	Beech Road
157?	Bokaro
156	The Illiad
155	Jinxy Jack
153?	Battalion
153	Athy Spirit
152	Sabin du Loir
152	Sondrio
151?	Al Asoof
151?	Fidway
151	Floyd
151	Royal Derbi
150	Cloughtaney
150	Yaheeb
149p	Oh So Risky
149	Jimbalou
149	Stratford Ponds
149	Sybillin
149	Yorkshire Holly
148p	Granville Again
148	Aldino
148	Deep Sensation
148	Henry Mann
148	Randolph Place
147P	Destriero
147?	Nordic Surprise
147	Norton's Coin
147	Pragada
147	Ryde Again
146	Judges Fancy
146	Upton Park
145p	Crystal Spirit
145	Philosophos
145	Riverhead
145	Welsh Bard
144 +	Mutare
144	Father Time
142?	Vayrua
142	Gran Alba
142	Sherwood Gunner
141	Danny Harrold
141	Gay Ruffian
141	Leading Role
141	Pipers Copse
141	Reve de Valse
141	Tyrone Bridge
141	Vagador
141	Wishlon
140p	Montpelier Lad
140p	Precious Boy
140p	Young Pokey
140 +	Fragrant Dawn
140	Brabazon
140	Danny Connors
140	Do Be Brief
140	Super Sense
140	Westway
139p	Mounamara
139	Gaasid
139	Honest Word
139	Major Inquiry
139	Rare Holiday
139	Rositary
138p	Better Times Ahead
138p	Winnie The Witch
138?	Past Glories

138	Black Humour	137	Coworth Park	136	Young Ty
138	Clifton Chapel	137	Jungle Knife	135p	Jodami
138	General Idea	137	Runway Romance	135p	South Harvest
138	Joyful Noise	137	Smith's Cracker	135	Bally Rue
138	State Jester	137	Windbound Lass	135	Chirkpar
137p	Minorettes Girl	136	Calabrese	135	Lacken Beau
137	Atlaal	136	Catch The Cross	135	Orbis
137	Bawnmore Lad	136	Lumberjack		

THE TIMEFORM
TOP NOVICES, JUVENILES
AND HUNTER CHASERS

Here are listed the 'Top 20' Novice Hurdlers, Novice Chasers, Juvenile Hurdlers and Hunter Chasers

Novice Hurdlers

167	Ruling
148p	Granville Again
147P	Destriero
147	Norton's Coin
146	Upton Park
142	Gran Alba
141	Tyrone Bridge
140p	Young Pokey
140	Danny Connors
140	Super Sense
139	Gaasid
138p	Better Times Ahead
138	General Idea
137p	Minorettes Girl
137	Jungle Knife
137	Smith's Cracker
135p	Jodami
135p	South Harvest
134	Book of Gold
133	Derring Valley

Novice Chasers

153p	Remittance Man
151p	Young Benz
150p	Sparkling Flame
149§	Redundant Pal
147	Uncle Ernie
141	Garamycin
141	Last 'o' The Bunch
140p	Rolling Ball
137?	Copperite
137	Esha Ness
137	Whats The Crack
136	Devil's Valley
136	Golden Celtic
136	Pat's Jester
135p	Good For A Laugh
135	Orbis
135	Rawhide
133	High Knowl
133	Trefelyn Cone
132+	Final Tub

Juvenile Hurdlers

149p	Oh So Risky
147?	Nordic Surprise
145p	Crystal Spirit
141	Reve de Valse
140p	Montpelier Lad
139p	Mounamara
137	Runway Romance
135	Chirkpar
134	Boarding School
133	Hopscotch
132	Native Mission
131	Silken Fan
131	Viking Flagship
129	Galevilla Express
128	Olympian
126	Legal Beagle
124	Arial Star
121p	Eurolink The Lad
121	Tim Soldier
120p	Bootscraper

Hunter Chasers

143?	Mystic Music
141	Field Conqueror
134	Lovely Citizen
132p	Cool It A Bit
129+	Dun Gay Lass
127?	High Ham Blues
126?	Lean Ar Aghaidh
126	Rawyards Brig
123	Crammer
122	Certain Light
120	Perroquet
120§	Risk A Bet
119	John Sam
119	Sanballat
118	Air Strike
118x	Old Nick
118	The Argonaut
117	Polar Glen
116p	Mount Argus
116	Run And Skip

THE BEST OF CHASERS & HURDLERS

The top performers of last season discussed by Timeform handicapper Simon Rowlands

For the fifth time running Desert Orchid is Timeform's most highly-rated horse of the jumps season. Whilst his rating of 178 is some way below his best of 187, he's clearly no back number yet. Two of his performances in the latest season left no room for argument on that score—his twelve-length defeat of Toby Tobias in Kempton's King George VI Rank Chase and his narrow victory in Sandown's Agfa Diamond Handicap Chase. The superlative merit of the former (by our reckoning the best effort in a non-handicap for several years) was plain for all to see. What seems to have been appreciated less is that Desert Orchid performed to a similar level at Sandown, where he ran off an official handicap mark of 177 (by a long chalk the highest any horse won off in the latest season) and conceded 15 lb to the high-class Nick The Brief. Of course, the true magnitude of Desert Orchid's achievements cannot be reflected in terms of figures alone. His durability is quite remarkable as well (he was our top-rated novice hurdler as long ago as the 1983/4 season), as is his versatility. For the third season in succession Desert Orchid also put up probably the best effort by a chaser over two miles when a close last-of-four finishers in the Victor Chandler Handicap at Ascot, conceding lumps of weight to his rivals who included the subsequent Queen Mother Champion Chase winner Katabatic.

Agfa Diamond Handicap Chase—Sandown

The steeplechasing scene will be much the poorer when Desert Orchid retires, as seems likely, in the coming season, but there are several exciting prospects around who'll be bidding to take over from where he left off. Chief amongst these, in our view, is Remittance Man. His rating of 153p shows that he still has a long way to go before he can be spoken of as one of the greats of recent years, but, frankly, we'll be disappointed if he doesn't manage just that. Very few novice chasers have impressed so much with the speed and accuracy of their jumping as did Remittance Man in the latest season. What is more, he put up his best effort—the best by a novice chaser all term—over a trip we consider to be short of his optimum when beating Uncle Ernie by six lengths in the two-mile Waterford Castle Arkle Challenge Trophy at Cheltenham. Against stiffer opposition (the leading novices are seldom tested sufficiently by their contemporaries to justify ratings much higher than Remittance Man's) and returned to trips of two and a half miles plus, Remittance Man seems sure to improve markedly on his rating—an eventuality implied by the p on his current figure.

It's probable that Remittance Man will run into Blazing Walker at least once in the coming season, and that horse will surely prove a tough nut for him to crack. Blazing Walker earned his rating of 173 (bettered by only Desert Orchid amongst the chasers) with his scintillating ten-length defeat of Katabatic in Aintree's two-and-a-half-mile Glenlivet Melling Chase, a race which also confirmed suspicions that the other leading shorter-distance chasers weren't an outstanding bunch. Given the style of Blazing Walker's success that day, it's possible we haven't seen the best of him yet either.

Other promising individuals on show at Aintree in April included the good novice chasers Young Benz and Sparkling Flame. On a line through Uncle Ernie, the former comes out only marginally behind Remittance Man at this stage, and we're hopeful that he'll improve into a leading contender for the Queen Mother Champion Chase in 1992. The honest if unspectacular Sparkling Flame staked his claim to the number-one spot amongst a slightly disappointing crop of staying novice chasers when handing out a bigger beating to Esha Ness in the Mumm Club Novices' Chase than had the promising but injury-prone Rolling Ball in the Sun Alliance Novices' Chase at the Cheltenham Festival.

There are other proven top-notchers against whom these up-and-coming performers may be judged, not least of them the Tote Cheltenham Gold Cup one-two Garrison Savannah and The Fellow. In our view this pair are well up to usual Gold Cup winning standard, their Timeform ratings of 171 being almost exactly the average achieved by the previous ten years' winners of chasing's blue riband. The Fellow won subsequently in the best company in his native France, while Garrison Savannah looked set more or less to confirm his Gold Cup rating in the Seagram Grand National until faltering dramatically after the last. Garrison Savannah and The Fellow are stouter stayers than many of those mentioned previously and should provide a stern test for future Gold Cup aspirants.

The previous year's Gold Cup winner, Norton's Coin, slipped down the chase ratings from 168 to 161§. We saw both sides of Norton's Coin's character in the 1990/1 season; his victory over Waterloo Boy late on at Cheltenham being the good, his earlier refusal in Ireland and throwing away of an easy opportunity at Aintree being the bad. It would be premature to write off Norton's Coin as a contender for the leading prizes, but, as the § attached to his rating denotes, we feel he's not one to rely on at present.

The hunter chase division, as is to be expected, was much weaker. Even by usual standards it was not well contested, with Lovely Citizen (Cheltenham's Christies Foxhunter) and Double Turn (Aintree's Seagram Fox Hunters') the most lowly-rated winners of their respective major races in the last decade. The previous year's leading hunter chaser Mystic Music gave every indication of being as good as ever with three easy victories prior to sustaining a serious injury in May. She generally beat little in 1991, however, and precisely what rating she was worth is open to doubt—a doubt indicated by the question mark on her figure.

Sandeman Hurdle—Liverpool

Prospects amongst the hurdlers for the coming season are almost as exciting. Overall, Timeform ratings for the best hurdlers are not quite so high as those for their chasing counterparts. One of the reasons for this is the tendency of many owners and trainers to switch their horses to fences before they have had sufficient opportunity to prove just how good they might become over the smaller obstacles. Such a story could have been Morley Street's. The season's outstanding hurdler—rated 162p at the outset—was returned to timber only after a campaign over fences that started promisingly but tailed off markedly. Chasing's loss was hurdling's gain, for Morley Street went on to prove himself one of the very best hurdlers of recent times with decisive victories in the Smurfit Champion Hurdle at Cheltenham and the Sandeman Hurdle at Aintree. It was Morley Street's win in the latter, in which he extended his superiority over the Cheltenham runner-up Nomadic Way from one and a half lengths to six, which earned him an annual Timeform rating of 174, the highest for a hurdler since Gaye Brief (rated 175) in the 1982/3 season. Perhaps, faced with even stronger opposition, Morley Street will end up being rated alongside the great hurdlers of the late-'seventies. Whatever, there seems no reason to believe that any of the other established hurdlers will prove equal to beating an on-song Morley Street at up to two and a half miles in 1991/2. His turn of foot and jumping ability set him apart from them in the latest season.

As with the chasers, amongst the hurdlers there are a number of highly-promising individuals working their way through the ranks. The leading novice hurdler Ruling achieved an outstanding rating of 167 for a horse at his stage of its career when finishing third in the Champion Hurdle. Without wishing to take anything away from the horse, this fact in itself is somewhat misleading. Very few good novices are even given a chance of proving their worth against experienced championship performers, and as a result they inevitably have their ratings limited to an extent by the 'ordinary' nature of their opposition. In this respect, Ruling has already realised more of his potential than have most of his contemporaries. He may prove capable of better still but hasn't the scope for improvement of the likes of Granville Again and Destriero, for instance. These two met in the Trafalgar House Supreme Novices' Hurdle at Cheltenham, where Destriero landed a massive gamble for his owner in winning by four lengths. Granville Again met trouble in running that day and duly showed better form when defying a penalty in a valuable novice event at Aintree. Interestingly, Granville Again is rated 1 lb higher than was his brother—Morley Street, no less—at the same stage of his career. Nonetheless, the impression we gained at Cheltenham was that Destriero would prove the better. His was a tremendous performance for one of such little experience (it was only his second outing over hurdles) and he travelled through the race like a very good horse indeed, scarcely making a mistake along the way. It's our view that Destriero will improve substantially on his present rating, and the P next to his figure of 147 indicates as much. He, above all others, could be the one to make Morley Street look to his laurels at Cheltenham in March.

Many felt they'd seen a future Champion Hurdler when Oh So Risky ran away with the Triumph Hurdle at Cheltenham in March. There hasn't been a more impressive winner of the race in more than two decades under its sponsorship by the Daily Express, and Oh So Risky couldn't reasonably have been expected to have done more than beat Chirkpar, as he did, by twelve lengths. Such remarks must be qualified, however. Overall there was less strength in depth amongst the leading juvenile hurdlers than is usual, and most of the very best representatives did not run in the Triumph in any case. In addition, the subsequent efforts of those who finished behind Oh So Risky did little to uphold the form. Even so, Oh So Risky's rating of 149p is the highest by a winner of the race since Meladon (also 149) in 1977, though we feel forced to reserve judgement about his Champion Hurdle chances until he's proved himself against stronger opposition. The Glenlivet Anniversary Hurdle at Aintree and its past equivalents have sometimes turned up a better juvenile performance than has been seen in the Triumph, but that wasn't the case in 1991. The winner of the race was Montpelier Lad, another horse of considerable promise, but one who, in terms of form at least, doesn't rank alongside the best recent winners.

Bishops Cleeve Hurdle—Cheltenham

Arguably the most promising of the other leading juvenile hurdlers was Crystal Spirit. He's a quite different type from Oh So Risky and Montpelier Lad, being very much a stayer, one who'll be seen to even better effect when tried beyond two and a half miles. At that trip Crystal Spirit was good enough in any case to beat older and more experienced rivals at Cheltenham in the Bishops Cleeve Hurdle in January and the Sun Alliance Novices' Hurdle in March. With the two leading staying hurdlers of the latest season, King's Curate and Run For Free, likely to be sent novice chasing in 1991/2, Crystal Spirit looks to have bright prospects of making a big impact in that sphere, with the Stayers' Hurdle at the next Festival an obvious target.

In conclusion, there seems good cause to look back on the 1990/1 National Hunt season with satisfaction and to view the coming campaign with greater than usual anticipation. It is in the nature of racing that many of the expected stars will fail to emerge, many of the hoped-for encounters will fail to take place. But, if even a fraction of the potential of the 1991/2 season is realised, then we're surely all in for a treat!

Timeform ratings are compiled daily and updated continually in the light of events. They represent an expression in terms of pounds of the merit of a horse's form as shown on the racecourse after all relevant details, such as weight carried, distance beaten, strength of opposition and so on, have been taken into account. These ratings are

	Two-Mile Chaser		Staying Chaser		Novice Chaser		Hunter Chaser
1990/1	178	Desert Orchid	178	Desert Orchid	153p	Remittance Man	143?	Mystic Music
1989/0	187	Desert Orchid	187	Desert Orchid	152p	Celtic Shot	143	Mystic Music
1988/9	182	Desert Orchid	182	Desert Orchid	169p	Carvill's Hill	142p	Call Collect
1987/8	174	Pearlyman	177	Desert Orchid	156p	Danish Flight	147	Certain Light
1986/7	171	Pearlyman	177	Desert Orchid	151p	Kildimo	146	Observe
1985/6	167	Dawn Run	183	Burrough Hill Lad	150	Pearlyman	148	Ah Whisht
1984/5	164+	Bobsline	184	Burrough Hill Lad	159	Druma-downey	141	Further Thought
1983/4	177	Badsworth Boy	175	Burrough Hill Lad	161p	Bobsline	149	Venture To Cognac
1982/3	179	Badsworth Boy	177	Bregawn	150	Righthand Man	147	Eliogarty
1981/2	170	Rathgorman	175	Silver Buck	147p	Brown Chamberlain	142	Compton Lad
1980/1	171	Anaglogs Daughter	176	Little Owl	145	Clayside	169	Spartan Missile
1979/0	163	I'm A Driver	171	Silver Buck	156	Anaglogs Daughter	132	Rolls Rambler
1978/9	151	Siberian Sun	166	Gay Spartan	151	Silver Buck	133+	Spartan Missile
1977/8	154	Tingle Creek	164	Midnight Court	145	The Dealer	133	Spartan Missile
1976/7	156	Skymas	163	Bannow Rambler	159§	Tree Tangle	124	Under Way
1975/6	167	Lough Inagh	182	Captain Christy	152p	Bannow Rambler	143	Otter Way

on a universal scale—from below 60 for the worst horses worthy of a rating to above 170 for the very best—so that comparisons can be made between horses who have no direct link of form. As an example, the form of any horse rated 110 is considered to be 10 lb superior to that shown by any horse rated 100.

Great care is taken at the end of each season to adjust the level of Timeform ratings to an annual 'mean'. The outcome of this is that Timeform ratings can be compared from one season to another, placing a horse's performances not only in an immediate but also in an historical context. Below is a list of Timeform Champions since the *Chasers & Hurdlers* annuals began in 1975/76, so that comparisons of this type may be made.

		Two-Mile Hurdler		Staying Hurdler		Novice Hurdler		Juvenile Hurdler
1990/1	174	Morley Street	164	King's Curate	167	Ruling	149p	Oh So Risky
1989/0	169	Kribensis	159	Trapper John	151	Regal Ambition	138	Sybillin
1988/9	172	Beech Road	169	Rustle	152p 152+	Sondrio Wishlon	144	Royal Derbi
1987/8	170	Celtic Shot	160	Galmoy	157p	Carvill's Hill	143p	Kribensis
1986/7	173	See You Then	165	Galmoy	153p	The West Awake	154	Aldino
1985/6	173	See You Then	167	Gaye Brief	158p	River Ceiriog	153p	Dark Raven
1984/5	172	Browne's Gazette	162	Bajan Sunshine	148p	Asir	151	Out of The Gloom
1983/4	173	Dawn Run	173	Dawn Run	158	Desert Orchid	142	Northern Game
1982/3	175	Gaye Brief	175	Gaye Brief	168	Dawn Run	147p	Sabin du Loir
1981/2	174	For Auction	171	Daring Run	149	Angelo Salvini	141	Shiny Copper
1980/1	175	Sea Pigeon	171+	Daring Run	159	Dunaree	144	Broadsword
1979/0	175	Sea Pigeon	167	Pollardstown	143	Slaney Idol	144	Hill of Slane
1978/9	180	Monksfield	180	Monksfield	162	Venture To Cognac	141	Pollardstown
1977/8	177	Monksfield	177	Monksfield	176	Golden Cygnet	144	Major Thompson
1976/7	182	Night Nurse	182	Night Nurse	154	Outpoint	149	Meladon
1975/6	178	Night Nurse	170	Comedy of Errors	159	Grand Canyon	157	Valmony

FOLLOW FRANCOME

Usually referred to by one of his fellow presenters on Channel 4 Racing as 'greatest jockey', John Francome rode 1,138 winners over jumps in Britain from 1969 until his retirement sixteen years later. Champion Jockey outright on six occasions—he shared the title with Peter Scudamore in 1981/2—Francome's numerous big-race successes included the 1978 Cheltenham Gold Cup on Midnight Court and the 1981 Champion Hurdle on Sea Pigeon.

I suppose you could say that almost every season drifts into life noticed only by real enthusiasts. It might be slightly different now compared to when I was last riding, in the 'eighties, as Martin Pipe's achievements rightly attract considerable attention. But a lot of the early jumping fixtures still take place with little interest from the Press. To a certain extent it's the same towards the end of each campaign, too. Last season finished just four days before the Derby, so not surprisingly that race took the lion's share of the racing media's attention. It used to irk me that approximately ten months of slogging round the country often merited only a paragraph or two on the back pages of the racing papers and, if at all, a line or two in the dailies. I'll never forget Jonjo O'Neill's record-breaking season in 1977/8. He was riding freelance, based in the North of England, yet managed a hundred and forty-nine winners. In pre-Pipe/Scudamore days that was unbelievable —in my view the equivalent of winning three gold medals at the Olympics. Yet it warranted only a tiny little piece on the back of the papers the next day. I just feel it was sad that a remarkable achievement didn't get anything like the recognition it deserved.

Although a lot of the early racing is moderate every jockey is raring to go from the first day. For all Scu's hundreds of winners and titles I can assure you he'll have been chuffed to get his first winner of the season, The Blue Boy at Newton Abbot, under his belt. No matter how successful you've been jump racing's an unpredictable sport, and none of the jockeys or trainers take anything for granted. Jump jockeys, generally speaking, are born optimists; given the nature of their business I suppose that's not surprising. The Pipes and Scudamores will be hoping for even greater achievements than before, whilst for lesser known and so far less successful trainers and jockeys a new season is, so to speak, the chance to begin again with the slate wiped clean.

The better quality horses don't begin to appear until the end of September, early-October, when Cheltenham and Chepstow offer some decent prizes. Until then southern-based riders have basically half a dozen or so tracks staging fixtures where there might be a chance of rides: Newton Abbot, Devon, Plumpton, Worcester, Fontwell and Hereford provide the majority of opportunities. In my early days I found this part of the season very frustrating. As a jockey who always struggled to some extent with my weight, having a ride at one meeting and then, because of a lack of racing and small fields for the races that were run, nothing for, say, another four days meant that riding at my minimum was hard. You've got to be exceptionally dedicated to starve yourself through periods like that. When I became successful obviously I was more in demand and it became less of a problem. But any jockey who has to waste to make a weight will confirm my view. It's okay when you're consistently busy but murder when you're not. So far as jump racing is concerned August is the month that highlights the folly in our system of allotting fixtures. Look at the nineteenth to the twenty-fourth. During that week there were just four meetings—two of them on Saturday; by then the season's been under way a month! I feel strongly that the season could begin later and end earlier. By fitting in the same number of fixtures you would avoid those weeks with just a couple of meetings here and there.

Although one's dealing mainly with moderate horses almost no jockey turns down rides; even if you've got a big stable to ride for later on you want to be involved straightaway. These days Martin Pipe provides Scu with lots of excellent chances but look at Richard Dunwoody or Graham McCourt, they'll ride almost anything offered. Although I was lucky enough to get quite a few early winners from John Jenkins I had the same attitude. Most jocks will let 'any dog bite once'! If I'm honest, more than once at Newton Abbot I popped a three-year-old that I hadn't schooled over hurdles on the way to the start, just to make sure that the trainer's assurance that it could jump was correct. I wasn't the only one to do so either! One day at Chepstow I rode a horse for Tim Forster in a novice chase. It felt a bit spooky on the way down so I put him over a fence—fortunately he was okay. I feel quite strongly that jockeys should be given a hurdle or fence to 'pop' on the way to the start. They are allowed to do so in France and, let's face it, show jumpers spend hours jumping yet just before a competition they warm up over obstacles in a separate ring; it's common sense.

One of the most striking reminders that the season is beginning to get into full swing comes in October when a jockey finds himself coming to the first in a novice chase at Cheltenham, Newbury or Ascot. The fences on these tracks are much stiffer and wider and, if you like, more of a test than a jockey has faced so far. If he hasn't got much confidence in his ride his concentration certainly sharpens! The ground almost everywhere at this time of the year is very fast: therefore an occasional shower at the likes of Ascot or Cheltenham quickly makes the ground a bit greasy. Horses who slip or lose their footing on occasions like this can have their confidence ruined. Funnily enough, quite often you'll find that an accident like this affects a horse who's been going nicely at the likes of Worcester or Newton Abbot, where the fences aren't so demanding, than, say, a newcomer beginning his chasing career. The horse with a bit of experience is suddenly faced with bigger fences which makes him think: added to that he isn't expecting to lose his footing either. At this time of year novices at Ascot and Newbury are, generally speaking, from the bigger yards where there are usually better schooling facilities. Up till then quite a lot of the horses from the smaller yards, even those horses that have been winning, haven't been schooled over much more than a few logs.

So far as picking winners goes, the less competitive the racing is the more chance you have. Admittedly there aren't many big-priced ones, particularly early on in the season, but there are opportunities in those first six to eight weeks to back winners. Since I finished riding I've been surprised to notice that simply by standing at the side of the paddock you can eliminate quite a number of horses on the score of fitness, or should I say, lack of it; they stand out like sore thumbs.

We're now into September and I suppose the season has begun to take shape in the way the majority of us expected—with Peter Scudamore and Martin Pipe dominating. Unless a catastrophe strikes they'll be champions in their respective fields once again. Although there were a number of successful conditional riders last season I didn't see one who impressed me particularly. Jamie Osborne, Oliver Sherwood's jockey, is still the best of the younger brigade but he doesn't have the support outside of Oliver's stable to trouble Peter Scudamore or even Richard Dunwoody.

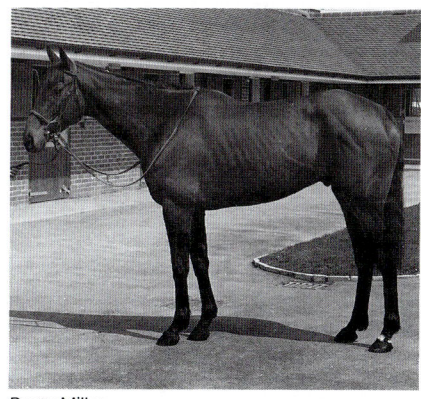

Dusty Miller

Finally, apart from wishing you all a most successful season, I mustn't forget my horses to follow. Firstly, I'm very much looking forward to watching Dusty Miller, trained by Simon Sherwood, in action once again. He's a horse that, in my opinion, is open to an enormous amount of improvement. For one that was basically a big weak baby he did amazingly well over hurdles last season. Apparently Simon will keep him to hurdles

Lonsdale Stakes, York—Supreme Choice from Retouch and Bondstone

until Christmas and then make a decision as to whether he'll go chasing. My other choices will probably surprise a few of you; both are trained by Barry Hills and, up until now, have run only on the Flat, Supreme Choice and Further Flight. Barry leases a yard from me, and so I know quite a lot of his horses really well. I've schooled both these for Barry in my indoor ring, and I can assure you they are natural jumpers; I was most impressed with them. Supreme Choice will, all being well, run in juvenile hurdles; he's a big horse with plenty of scope. Further Flight could, with a bit of luck, do just as well, if not better, than Nomadic Way. For a start he's a much faster type, one who's well able to lie up with some of Barry's sprinters at home, and he's got the kindest temperament; I love him.

Further Flight

Hambleton Thoroughbred Racing 1989 plc

Dear Racing Enthusiast,

Have you ever thought how much extra interest could be derived from limited involvement in the ownership of horses?

I have been running successful Flat Racing Syndicates for several years and understand the importance of personal contacts if the maximum pleasure and profit is to be achieved. My members have benefited from good information, both on our own horses and, of course others, where I have connections. One of the main reasons for our success has been the small number of people involved and I do not intend to change this. However, we always have a few vacancies at this time of year for additional members.

If you are genuinely interested in participating in the ownership of around a dozen horses (trained in Newmarket and Yorkshire), and the consequent benefits, please ring or write to me at the address below.

Yours sincerely,

Peter Lewis

PS: *My members landed several nice touches this summer with our own horses.*

BELLEFAN	**16/1 to 6/1,**	Kempton
BELLEFAN	**7/2 to 2/1,**	Brighton
GOVERNOR'S IMP	**16/1**	Haydock
MERCHANT OF VENICE	**5/1**	Southwell
MERCHANT OF VENICE	**9/1**	Lingfield

All clearly recommended through our daily information service.

MOWBRAY COTTAGE, AMPLEFORTH, NORTH YORKSHIRE YO6 4DX. TEL: 04393 726 FAX: 04393 228
Directors: P.N.G. Lewis, M.H.G. Lewis, M.E.B. Lewis, W.J.P. Jackson. Registered Office: 62, Wilson Street, London EC2A 2BU
Registered in England No. 2307561

TIMEFORM RACEVIEW
Daily Previews and Analysis

Raceview is Timeform's 0898 line. It started life as a single service, previewing the pick of the day's events, but was quickly expanded to include a full race-by-race analysis of the day's two most important meetings. Its compilers work direct from the Timeform Race Card, sifting through one meeting apiece plus a share of the minor meetings. For Raceview, the overnight service, it's the more prestigious events, pattern races and valuable handicaps, that tend to be scrutinized first, but naturally these races don't always provide a ready-made winner, so the Raceview may open up with a more confident selection from a lesser race.

Top-rated horses are given priority when selections are made, but ratings aren't the be all and end all, of course. For every runner with an outstanding chance at the weights, it's necessary to check whether it'll be suited by the trip, the ground and the track, for example. Again, the Race Card will provide the answers here via the Timeform comments. Fitness must be considered too, along with other factors such as draw, jockeyship and tactics, but if everything fits into place, bingo—the writer is away.

Raceview is broadcast from 5.30pm, but the script has to be written, typed and checked by about four. It lasts only three to four minutes, but the readers need time to become acquainted with it before recording. It's important for them to voice accurately the drift of the case being argued if the listener is to be left in no doubt as to how the land lies.

On the overnight line, the script will usually leave the listener to his own devices when it comes to backing the selection. Whether to take an early price, or indeed whether to bet at all once the market is known. Things are different on the morning line. By the time the Race-by-Raceview is broadcast—the first meeting at 10.15 and the second at 10.45—the odds are more widely available. Betting is all about obtaining value, of course, and Raceview's prime concern is to steer the listener in the right direction, away from a 'bad' favourite or onto a 'lively' outsider.

As an example, here's the script for the Schweppes Mile at Goodwood on August 1 *The £100,000 Schweppes Golden Mile at three forty five is usually one of the season's most keenly-contested handicaps, but according to the layers this year's renewal is practically a two-horse race. Favourite is Michael Stoute's Desert Dirham, who made all to beat Desert Sun by one and a half lengths at Yarmouth last month, after the weights for this race were published, and he looks something of a handicap snip with just 8-10 today. However, that was only Desert Dirham's second appearance in public, and his inexperience could certainly count against him in the hurly-burly of a big field round this sharp mile, so current quotes of around 9/4 don't appeal. The other outstanding contender here is John Sutcliffe's Superoo, who had no* sort of run until inside the final furlong when a most unlucky second to Savoyard in the Bunbury Cup at Newmarket last time. His best form to date is at seven furlongs, but it's far from conclusive that this longer trip is beyond him, and off bottom weight he must have every chance of repeating his stable's win in this race twelve months ago with March Bird. With it possible to get 16/1 the field outside Desert Dirham and Superoo there should be some each-way value around, and one who could give you a run for your money at a long price is Reg Akehurst's Sky Cloud. Sky Cloud has already won one valuable handicap this season, Ascot's Victoria Cup by three lengths from Band On The Run, and, while he's gone up the weights since, the likely strong gallop will suit him here, as will the prevailing easy ground. SKY CLOUD WON 20-1

PRINCIPAL LINE

0898·330·330

THE FULL TIMEFORM RACEVIEW SERVICE.

Raceview — A preview of the best of the day's racing, available from early the previous evening.

Race-by-Raceview — A race-by-race view of the two main meetings, starting half an hour before the first race. Concise analysis of the next race at each meeting.

FIRST MEETING

0898·330·100

Full race-by-race preview and analysis of the day's main meeting (from 10.15 am).

Individual Raceviews (from 10.15 am) — Dial (0898) 330101 for first-race preview, (0898) 330102 for second race, and so on.

SECOND MEETING

0898·330·200

Full race-by-race preview of the day's second meeting (from 10.45 am).

Individual Raceviews (from 10.45 am) — Dial (0898) 330201 for first-race preview, (0898) 330202 for second race, and so on.

HORSES TO NOTE

0898·330·350

Horses specially noted by our race-readers plus specific ante-post advice

TELEVIEW

0898·330·321

The Timeform Raceview analysis of all races televised by BBC and Channel 4. Available from 10.30 am.

Dial 0898 330399 for your FREE Timeform Raceview wallet card

Calls are charged at 36p per minute 'cheap' rate and 48p per minute at all other times

Timeform Raceview is a service from the Timeform Organisation.

FIXTURES 1991/92

(a) Denotes all-weather jumping meeting
(aF) Denotes all-weather Flat meeting
* Denotes evening meeting

October

1 Tue.	Devon & Exeter
2 Wed.	Cheltenham, Sedgefield
3 Thu.	Cheltenham
4 Fri.	Hexham
5 Sat.	Chepstow, Kelso, Uttoxeter
7 Mon.	Southwell
8 Tue.	Newton Abbot
9 Wed.	Plumpton, Towcester
10 Thu.	Wincanton
11 Fri.	Carlisle, Market Rasen
12 Sat.	Ayr, Bangor, Southwell, Worcester
14 Mon.	Fontwell
15 Tue.	Devon & Exeter, Sedgefield
16 Wed.	Cheltenham, Wetherby
17 Thu.	Hexham, Taunton, Uttoxeter
18 Fri.	Ludlow
19 Sat.	Kelso, Kempton, Southwell, Stratford
21 Mon.	Fakenham
22 Tue.	Plumpton
23 Wed.	Ascot, Newcastle
24 Thu.	Southwell, Wincanton
25 Fri.	Devon & Exeter, Hereford, Newbury
26 Sat.	Catterick, Huntingdon, Worcester
30 Wed.	Fontwell, Sedgefield
31 Thu.	Kempton, Stratford

November

1 Fri.	Bangor, Wetherby
2 Sat.	Chepstow, Sandown, Warwick, Wetherby
4 Mon.	Plumpton, Wolverhampton
5 Tue.	Devon & Exeter, Hereford, Nottingham
6 Wed.	Kelso, Newbury
7 Thu.	Lingfield (aF), Uttoxeter, Wincanton
8 Fri.	Cheltenham, Hexham, Market Rasen
9 Sat.	Cheltenham, Newcastle, Windsor
11 Mon.	Carlisle, Wolverhampton
12 Tue.	Sedgefield, Southwell (aF)
13 Wed.	Haydock, Newbury, Worcester
14 Thu.	Ayr, Lingfield (aF), Taunton, Towcester
15 Fri.	Ascot, Ayr, Huntingdon
16 Sat.	Ascot, Ayr, Catterick, Warwick
18 Mon.	Bangor, Leicester, Windsor
19 Tue.	Newton Abbot, Nottingham, Southwell (aF), Wetherby
20 Wed.	Haydock, Kelso, Kempton
21 Thu.	Haydock, Ludlow, Wincanton
22 Fri.	Leicester, Newbury, Sedgefield
23 Sat.	Market Rasen, Newbury, Newcastle, Towcester
25 Mon.	Catterick, Folkestone, Wolverhampton
26 Tue.	Devon & Exeter, Huntingdon, Stratford
27 Wed.	Hereford, Hexham, Plumpton
28 Thu.	Carlisle, Lingfield (aF), Taunton, Warwick
29 Fri.	Bangor, Sandown, Southwell (aF)
30 Sat.	Chepstow, Nottingham, Sandown, Wetherby

December

2 Mon.	Kelso, Worcester
3 Tue.	Fontwell, Leicester, Newcastle
4 Wed.	Catterick, Huntingdon, Ludlow, Southwell (aF)
5 Thu.	Lingfield (aF), Taunton, Uttoxeter, Windsor
6 Fri.	Cheltenham, Devon & Exeter, Doncaster
7 Sat.	Cheltenham, Doncaster, Lingfield, Towcester
9 Mon.	Edinburgh, Warwick
10 Tue.	Plumpton, Sedgefield
11 Wed.	Haydock, Worcester
12 Thu.	Haydock, Southwell (aF)
13 Fri.	Catterick, Fakenham, Hereford
14 Sat.	Ascot, Edinburgh, Lingfield (aF), Nottingham
16 Mon.	Ludlow, Newton Abbot
17 Tue.	Folkestone, Southwell (aF)
18 Wed.	Bangor, Lingfield (aF)
19 Thu.	Kelso, Towcester
20 Fri.	Hereford, Hexham, Uttoxeter
21 Sat.	Chepstow, Edinburgh, Lingfield, Uttoxeter
26 Thu.	Huntingdon, Kempton, Market Rasen, Newton Abbot, Sedgefield, Wetherby, Wincanton, Wolverhampton
27 Fri.	Kempton, Lingfield (aF), Taunton, Wetherby, Wolverhampton
28 Sat.	Folkestone, Newbury, Newcastle, Southwell (aF), Stratford
30 Mon.	Carlisle, Fontwell, Newbury, Warwick
31 Tue.	Catterick, Cheltenham, Leicester, Plumpton

January

1 Wed.	Catterick, Cheltenham, Devon & Exeter, Leicester, Southwell (aF), Windsor
2 Thu.	Ayr, Lingfield (a), Nottingham
3 Fri.	Edinburgh, Newton Abbot, Southwell (aF)

4 Sat.	Haydock, Lingfield (aF), Market Rasen, Southwell
6 Mon.	Lingfield, Southwell (a), Wolverhampton
7 Tue.	Chepstow, Leicester, Lingfield (a)
8 Wed.	Kelso, Plumpton, Southwell (a)
9 Thu.	Edinburgh, Lingfield (a), Wincanton
10 Fri.	Ascot, Southwell (aF), Wetherby
11 Sat.	Ascot, Lingfield (aF), Market Rasen, Newcastle, Warwick
13 Mon.	Carlisle, Fontwell, Southwell (a)
14 Tue.	Folkestone, Lingfield (a), Sedgefield
15 Wed.	Ludlow, Southwell (aF), Windsor
16 Thu.	Lingfield (a), Taunton
17 Fri.	Catterick, Kempton, Southwell (aF), Towcester
18 Sat.	Catterick, Haydock, Kempton, Lingfield (aF), Warwick
20 Mon.	Leicester, Lingfield, Southwell (a)
21 Tue.	Chepstow, Lingfield (aF), Nottingham
22 Wed.	Sedgefield, Southwell (a), Wolverhampton
23 Thu.	Huntingdon, Lingfield (a), Newton Abbot
24 Fri.	Southwell (aF), Uttoxeter, Wincanton
25 Sat.	Ayr, Cheltenham, Doncaster, Lingfield (aF)
27 Mon.	Plumpton, Southwell (a)
28 Tue.	Leicester, Lingfield (a), Sedgefield
29 Wed.	Nottingham, Southwell (aF), Windsor
30 Thu.	Edinburgh, Lingfield (a), Towcester
31 Fri.	Kelso, Lingfield, Southwell (aF)

February

1 Sat.	Chepstow, Lingfield (aF), Sandown, Stratford, Wetherby
3 Mon.	Fontwell, Southwell (a), Wolverhampton
4 Tue.	Carlisle, Lingfield (aF), Warwick
5 Wed.	Ascot, Ludlow, Southwell (a)
6 Thu.	Huntingdon, Lingfield (a), Wincanton
7 Fri.	Bangor, Newbury, Sedgefield, Southwell (aF)
8 Sat.	Ayr, Catterick, Lingfield (aF), Newbury, Uttoxeter
10 Mon.	Hereford, Plumpton, Southwell (a)
11 Tue.	Lingfield (a), Newton Abbot, Towcester
12 Wed.	Folkestone, Southwell (aF), Worcester

13 Thu.	Leicester, Lingfield (a), Sandown, Taunton
14 Fri.	Edinburgh, Fakenham, Sandown, Southwell (aF)
15 Sat.	Chepstow, Lingfield (aF), Newcastle, Nottingham, Windsor
17 Mon.	Fontwell, Southwell (a), Wolverhampton
18 Tue.	Huntingdon, Lingfield (aF), Sedgefield
19 Wed.	Folkestone, Southwell (a), Warwick
20 Thu.	Catterick, Lingfield (a), Wincanton
21 Fri.	Kelso, Kempton, Southwell (aF)
22 Sat.	Doncaster, Edinburgh, Kempton, Lingfield (aF), Stratford
24 Mon.	Doncaster, Leicester, Southwell (a)
25 Tue.	Lingfield (a), Nottingham
26 Wed.	Plumpton, Southwell (aF), Wetherby, Worcester
27 Thu.	Lingfield (a), Ludlow
28 Fri.	Haydock, Newbury, Southwell (aF)
29 Sat.	Haydock, Hereford, Lingfield (aF), Market Rasen, Newbury

March

2 Mon.	Leicester, Southwell (a), Windsor
3 Tue.	Lingfield (aF), Sedgefield, Warwick
4 Wed.	Bangor, Catterick, Folkestone, Southwell (a)
5 Thu.	Lingfield (a), Stratford, Wincanton
6 Fri.	Carlisle, Market Rasen, Sandown, Southwell (aF)
7 Sat.	Ayr, Chepstow, Doncaster, Lingfield (aF), Sandown
9 Mon.	Plumpton, Southwell (a), Taunton
10 Tue.	Cheltenham, Lingfield (aF), Sedgefield
11 Wed.	Cheltenham, Newton Abbot
12 Thu.	Cheltenham, Hexham
13 Fri.	Fakenham, Lingfield, Wolverhampton
14 Sat.	Chepstow, Lingfield, Newcastle, Southwell (aF), Uttoxeter
16 Mon.	Newcastle, Wolverhampton
17 Tue.	Fontwell, Nottingham
18 Wed.	Kelso, Southwell (aF), Worcester
19 Thu.	Devon & Exeter, Towcester
20 Fri.	Ludlow, Newbury
21 Sat.	Bangor, Hexham, Lingfield (aF), Newbury
23 Mon.	Hexham
24 Tue.	Sandown
25 Wed.	Worcester

26 Thu.	Taunton
27 Fri.	Plumpton, Wincanton
28 Sat.	Ascot, Southwell
31 Tue.	Sedgefield

April

1 Wed.	Worcester
2 Thu.	Liverpool
3 Fri.	Devon & Exeter, Liverpool
4 Sat.	Hereford, Liverpool
6 Mon.	Kelso
7 Tue.	Southwell
8 Wed.	Ascot, Ludlow
9 Thu.	Taunton
10 Fri.	Ayr
11 Sat.	Ayr, Bangor, Stratford
13 Mon.	Huntingdon
14 Tue.	Fontwell, Sedgefield
15 Wed.	Cheltenham
16 Thu.	Cheltenham
18 Sat.	Carlisle, Newton Abbot, Plumpton, Southwell, Towcester
20 Mon.	Carlisle, Chepstow, Fakenham, Hereford, Huntingdon, Market Rasen, Newton Abbot, Plumpton, Towcester, Uttoxeter, Wetherby, Wincanton
21 Tue.	Chepstow, Uttoxeter, Wetherby
22 Wed.	Ludlow*, Perth
23 Thu.	Perth
24 Fri.	Perth, Taunton*
25 Sat.	Hexham, Market Rasen, Sandown, Worcester*
27 Mon.	Hexham*
28 Tue.	Ascot*, Sedgefield*
29 Wed.	Cheltenham*, Kelso

May

1 Fri.	Bangor*, Newton Abbot
2 Sat.	Hereford*, Hexham*, Uttoxeter
4 Mon.	Devon & Exeter, Fontwell, Haydock, Ludlow, Newcastle, Southwell, Towcester
5 Tue.	Chepstow, Sedgefield*
6 Wed.	Wetherby*, Worcester*
7 Thu.	Uttoxeter*
8 Fri.	Stratford*, Wincanton*
9 Sat.	Bangor, Market Rasen*, Newcastle*, Warwick*
12 Tue.	Folkestone*, Newton Abbot, Towcester*
13 Wed.	Hereford, Newton Abbot*, Perth*
14 Thu.	Huntingdon*, Perth
15 Fri.	Stratford*
16 Sat.	Warwick*
20 Wed.	Perth*, Worcester
22 Fri.	Towcester
23 Sat.	Cartmel, Hexham

24 Mon.	Cartmel, Fakenham, Fontwell, Hereford, Hexham*, Huntingdon, Uttoxeter, Wetherby
26 Tue.	Uttoxeter*
27 Wed.	Cartmel
29 Fri.	Stratford*
30 Sat.	Market Rasen*, Stratford